Picasso

1881-1973

Grange BOOKS

Page 4:
Pablo Picasso, Photograph, 1904
Dedicated to Suzanne and Henri Bloch

Designed by :
Baseline Co Ltd
19-25 Nguyen Hue
Bitexco Building, Floor 11
District 1, Ho Chi Minh City
Vietnam

ISBN 1-84013-732-0

Published in 2005 by Grange Books
an imprint of Grange Books Plc
The Grange Kingsnorth Industrial Estate
Hoo, nr Rochester, Kent ME3 9ND
www.grangebooks.co.uk

Printed in China

Foreword

"People want to find "meaning" in everything and everyone. That is the disease of our age, an age that is anything but practical but believes itself to be more pratical than any other age."

Picasso

À mes chers amis
Suzanne et Henri
Picasso
1904

Biography

1881:   Birth of Pablo Ruiz Picasso in Málaga. Parents: José Ruiz Blasco, a teacher of drawing at the School of Fine Arts and Crafts and curator of the local museum, and Maria Picasso y Lopez.

1888-89: The first of little Pablo's paintings, *Picador*.

1895:   In Madrid, at the Prado he discovers Velázquez and Goya. Enrols at the School of Fine Arts in Barcelona, popularly called "La Lonja". His father rents a studio for him. Paints his first large academic canvas, *First Communion*.

1899:   In Barcelona joins a group of avant-garde intellectual artists who frequent the café Els Quatre Gats. Modernist tendencies appear in his works. Paints *The Last Moments*.

1900:   *The Last Moments* is exhibited at the Paris Exposition Universelle.

1901:   Publishes the review Arte Joven. Development of pre-Fauvist style (Cabaret Period). Exhibition of 65 of his works at the Galerie Vollard. Friendship with Max Jacob. Influenced by Lautrec and Van Gogh. The *Casagemas* death cycle. First Blue paintings.

1902:   Develops Blue style in Barcelona.

1904:   Moves into the Bateau-Lavoir in Montmartre. End of Blue Period. Takes up engraving. Friendship with Apollinaire and Salmon. Meets Fernande Olivier.

1905:   Exhibits at Galerie Serrurier (travelling circus themes). Completes the large canvas *Family of Saltimbanques*. End of the Circus Period.

1906:   Rose Classicism. Gertrude Stein introduces Picasso to Matisse. Meets André Derain. Summer in Gosol. That autumn in Paris: paints a self-portrait reflecting Iberian archaic sculpture.

1907:   *Les Demoiselles d'Avignon*. That summer visits the ethnographic museum at Palais du Trocadéro, where he discovers for himself African sculpture. Meets Kahnweiler and Georges Braque.

1908:   Proto-Cubism. The term "Cubism" is born.

1909:   From May to September works in Horta de Ebro, develops Analytical Cubism.

1910:   "High" phase of Analytical Cubism. Nine works shown in London, in the Manet and the Post-Impressionists exhibition.

1912:   Makes his first collage, *Still-Life with Chair Caning*. Transition of Cubism to Synthetic phase. First papiers collés and constructions.

1914:   Rococo Cubism combines with Cubist structures in a foreshadowing of Surrealist methods.

1915:   "Ingres" portraits.

1917:   Joins the Diaghilev troupe in Rome, works on décor and costumes for the ballet Parade. Meets ballerina Olga Khokhlova (1891-1955).

1918:   Wedding of Picasso and Olga (12 July). Death of Apollinaire (9 November). Moves to 23, rue La Boétie.

1919:   Trip to London (May-August) : design décor and costumes for the ballet *Le Tricorne* (by Manuel de Falla).

1921:   Birth of son Paulo (4 February). Continues to work for Diaghilev (Cuadro Flamenco). Neo-Classicism.

1925:   Works in Monte Carlo for the Ballets Russes. Paints *The Dance*.

1927:   In January meets seventeen-year-old Marie-Thérèse Walter. Theme of biomorphic bathers. First etchings for *Le Chef-d'œuvre Inconnu* by Balzac.

1928:   Executes the huge collage Minotaur. Studio theme appears in his painting, and welded constructions in sculpture (aided by Julio González).

1930:   Crucifixion based on Matthias Grünewald's Isenheim Altarpiece. Series of etchings illustrating Ovid's *Metamorphoses*.

1932:   Major retrospective (236 works) in Paris and Zurich. Lives and works at Boisgeloup: "Biomorphic metamorphic" style. Zervos publishes the first volume of the Picasso Catalogue Raisonné.

PICASSO

1933: First issue of the Surrealist magazine Minotaure. Bullfight and female toreador themes. Fernande Olivier publishes her memoirs, *Picasso et Ses Amis*. Also published is Bernhard Geiser's *Catalogue Raisonné*.

1935: Engraves *Minotauromachy*. That summer completely abandons painting in favour of writing. Birth of Maia, daughter of Picasso and Marie-Thérèse Walter. Jaime Sabartés, becomes his companion and secretary.

1936: Friendship with Paul Eluard. Beginning of the Civil War in Spain (18 July); the Republican Government appoints him director of the Prado Museum. Meets Dora Maar, who becomes his mistress. Together they discover the town of Vallauris, a nearby ceramics centre.

1937: Finds new studio at 7, Rue de Grands-Augustins, where he works on Guernica throughout May.

1938: *Women at Their Toilette*. Series of seated women (Dora) and portraits of children (Maia).

1939: Death of Picasso's mother in Barcelona (13 January). Barcelona and Madrid fall. *Guernica* exhibited in America. Outbreak of World War II finds him in Paris. Leaves for Royan, where he stays, on and off, until December. Major retrospective, Picasso: Forty Years of His Art, at the Museum of Modern Art, New York.

1943: Makes the acquaintance of the young painter Françoise Gilot.

1945: Paints the anti-war *The Charnel House*. Is attracted to lithography: a portrait of Françoise Gilot.

1946: Painting *Monument aux Espagnols*. Begins living with François Gilot. The Palais Grimaldi, soon renamed the Musée Picasso; the themes include fauns, naiads, centaurs.

1947: Birth of Claude, first child of Françoise and Picasso (15 May). Takes up ceramics in Vallauris.

1948: Illustrations. Together with Eluard, flies to Wroclaw, Poland, for the Congress of Intellectuals for Peace; receives Commander's Cross with Star of the Order of the Renaissance of the Polish Republic. Exhibits 149 ceramics in November in Paris.

1949: Lithograph of a dove for the poster of the Peace Congress in Paris becomes known as the *Dove of Peace*. Birth of Paloma (19 April), daughter of Picasso and Françoise Gilot.

1950: Awarded the Peace Prize.

1951: Paints Massacre in Korea, exhibited in Salon de Mai, Paris. Most of the time lives in the Midi, works at Vallauris, visits Matisse in Nice.

1953: Major retrospectives in Rome, Milan, Lyons, São Paulo. Separation from Françoise Gilot.

1954: Drawings in *Painter* and *Model* series. Portrait of Jacqueline Roque. Series of paintings based on Delacroix's *Women of Algiers*.

1955: Major retrospective (150 works) at the Musée des Arts Decoratifs, Paris. Henri-Georges Clouzot's film *Le Mystère Picasso*.

1956: Major exhibitions in Moscow and St. Petersburg on the occasion of Picasso's 75th birthday.

1957: *The Maids of Honour (Las Meninas)*, after Velázquez.

1959: Begins long series of works on theme of Manet's *Déjeuner sur l'Herbe*.

1961: Wedding of Picasso and Jacqueline Roque.

1962: Awarded the Lenin Prize.

1963: Opening of Museo Picasso in Barcelona.

1966: Major retrospective in Paris in honour of 85th birthday.

1970: Picasso's relatives in Barcelona donate all paintings and sculptures to Museo Picasso, Barcelona. The Bateau-Lavoir destroyed by fire on 12 May.

1971: Exhibition in the Grand Gallery of the Louvre in honour of Picasso's 90th birthday.

1972: Prepares a new exhibition of his most recent works for the Palais des Papes in Avignon.

1973: Exhibition of 156 engravings at Galerie Louise Leiris, Paris. 8 April: Picasso dies at Notre-Dame-de-Vie in Mougins. Buried on 10 April in the grounds of the Château de Vauvenargues.

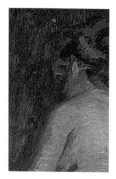

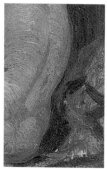

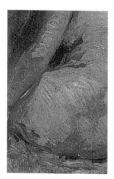

The works of Picasso published in the present volume cover those early periods which, based on considerations of style, have been classified as Steinlenian (or Lautrecian), Stained Glass, Blue, Circus, Rose, Classic, "African", Proto-Cubist, Cubist... From the viewpoint of the "science of man", these periods correspond to the years 1900-1914, when Picasso was between nineteen and thirty-three, the time which saw the formation and flowering of his unique personality.

Study of a Nude seen from the Back

1895
oil on wood, 22.3 x 13.7 cm
Museo Picasso, Barcelona

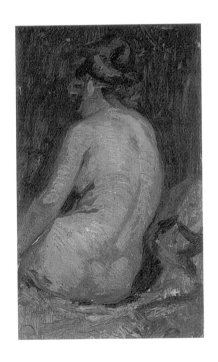

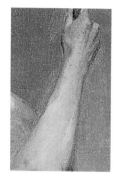

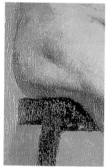

But a scientific approach to Picasso's œuvre has long been in use: his work has been divided into periods, explained both by creative contacts and reflections of biographical events. If Picasso's work has for us the general significance of universal human experience, this is due to the fact that it expresses, with the most exhaustive completeness, man's internal life and all the laws of its development.

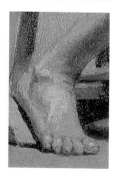

Academic Study

c. 1895-1897
oil on canvas, 82 x 61 cm
Museo Picasso, Barcelona

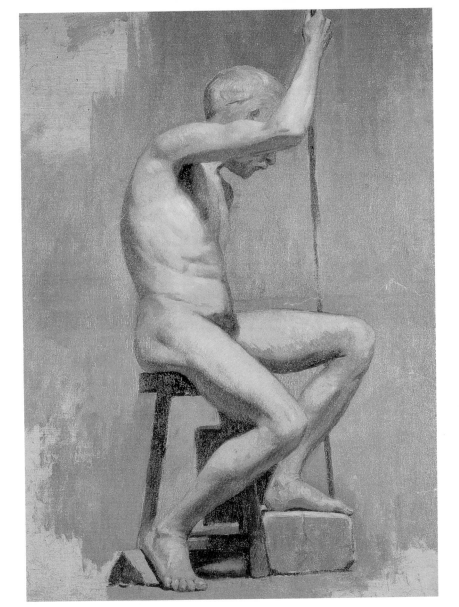

11

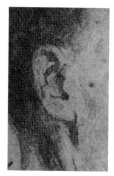

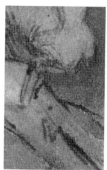

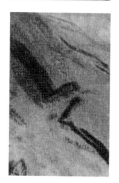

Only by approaching his œuvre in this way can we hope to understand its rules, the logic of its evolution, the transition from one putative period to another.

Picasso was born a Spaniard and, so they say, began to draw before he could speak. As an infant he was instinctively attracted to the artist's tools. In early childhood he could spend hours tracing his first pictures in the sand.

Portrait of the Artist's Father

1896
oil on canvas and cardboard, 42.3 x 30.8 cm
Museo Picasso, Barcelona

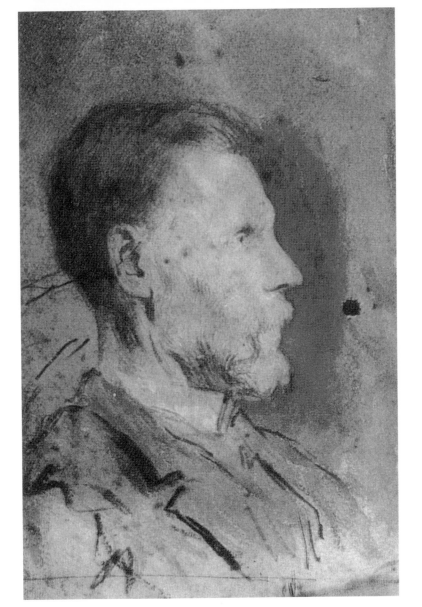

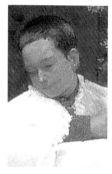

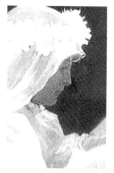

This early self-expression held the promise of a rare gift.

Málaga must be mentioned, for it was there, on 25 October 1881, that Pablo Ruiz Picasso was born and there that he spent the first ten years of his life. Málaga was the cradle of his spirit, the land of his childhood, the soil in which many of the themes and images of his mature work are rooted.

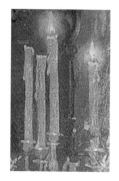

First Communion

1896
oil on canvas, 166 x 118 cm
Museo Picasso, Barcelona

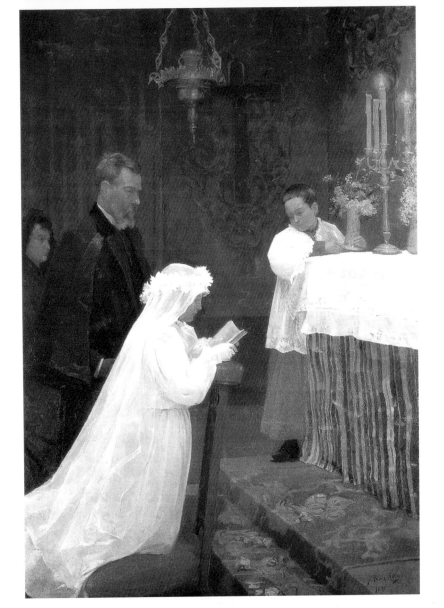

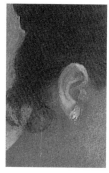

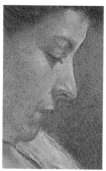

He first saw a picture of Hercules in Málaga's municipal museum, witnessed bullfights on the Plaza de Toros, and at home watched the cooing doves that served as models for his father.

The young Pablo drew all of this and by the age of eight took up brush and oils to paint a bullfight. As for school, Pablo hated it from the first day and opposed it furiously.

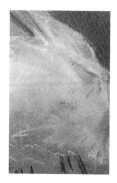

Portrait of the Artist's Mother

1896
pastel on paper, 19.5 x 12 cm
Museo Picasso, Barcelona

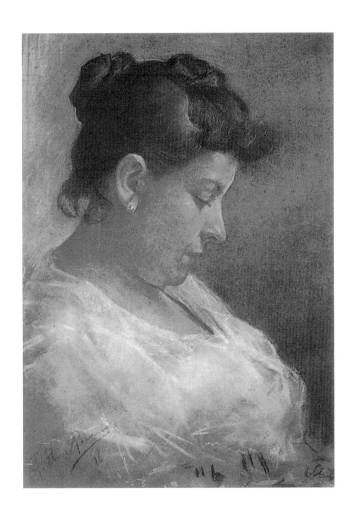

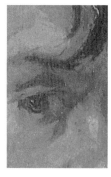

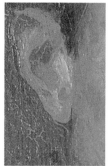

In 1891, financial difficulties forced the Ruiz Picasso family to move to La Coruña, where Pablo's father was offered a position as teacher of drawing and painting in a secondary school. La Coruña had a School of Fine Arts. There the young Pablo Ruiz began his systematic studies of drawing and with prodigious speed completed (by the age of thirteen!) the academic Plaster Cast and Nature Drawing Classes.

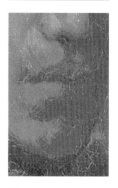

Self-Portrait

1896
oil on canvas, 32.7 x 23.6 cm
Museo Picasso, Barcelona

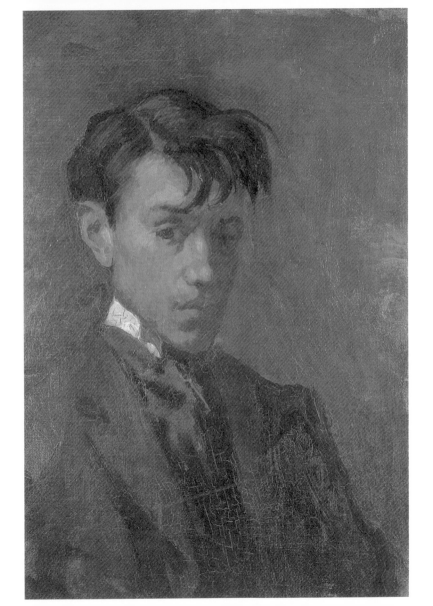

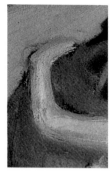

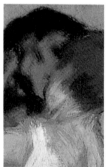

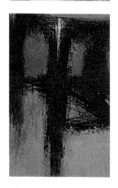

What strikes one most in his works from this time is not so much the phenomenal accuracy and exactitude of execution as what the young artist introduced into this frankly boring material: a treatment of light and shade that transformed the plaster torsos, hands and feet into living images of bodily perfection over-flowing with poetic mystery.

The Embrace

1900
oil on cardboard, 52 x 56 cm
The Pushkin Museum of Fine Arts, Moscow

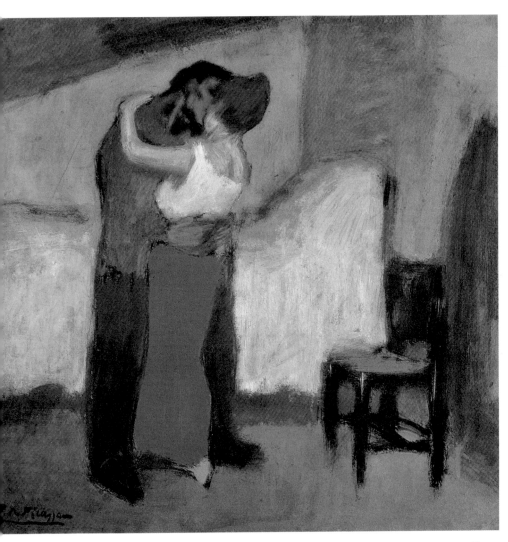

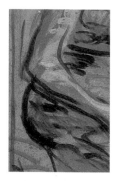

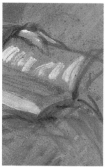

He did not, however, limit his drawing to the classroom; he drew at home, all the time, using whatever subject matter was at hand: portraits of the family, genre scenes, romantic subjects, animals. In keeping with the times, he "published" his own journals – *La Coruña* and *Azul y Blanco (Blue and White)* – writing them by hand and illustrating them with cartoons.

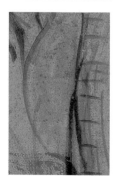

Woman Reading

1900
oil on cardboard, 56 x 52 cm
The Pushkin Museum of Fine Arts, Moscow

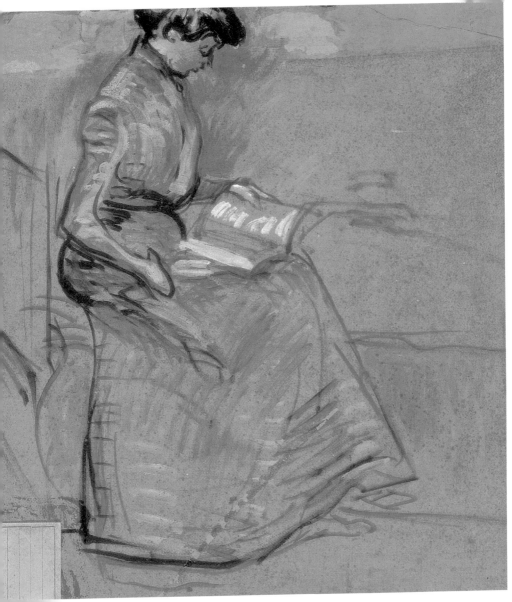

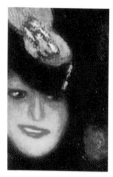

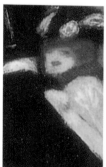

At home, under his father's tutelage during his last year in La Coruña, Pablo began to paint live models in oils (see *Portrait of an Old Man* and *Beggar in a Cap*).

These portraits and figures speak not only of the early maturity of the thirteen-year-old painter, but also of the purely Spanish nature of his gift: a preoccupation with human beings, whom he treated with profound seriousness and strict realism, uncovering the monolithic and "cubic" character of these images.

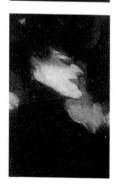

Le Moulin de la Galette

1900
oil on canvas, 90.2 x 117 cm
The Solomon R. Guggenheim Museum
Justin K. Thannhauser Foundation, New York

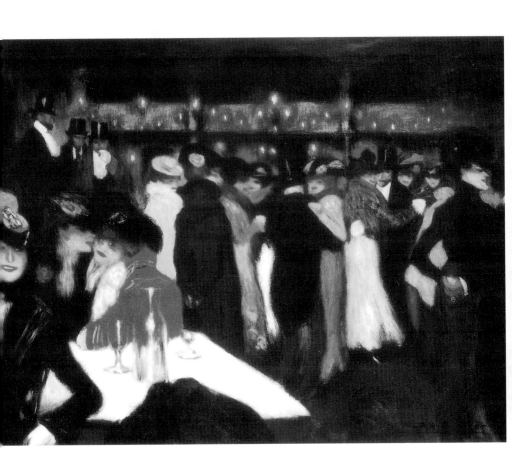

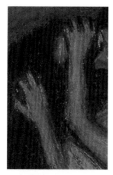

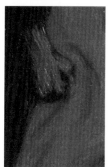

That is the way in which Picasso expressed how much his work was intertwined with his life; he also used the word "diary" with reference to his work. D.-H. Kahnweiler, who knew Picasso for over sixty-five years, wrote: "It is true that I have described his œuvre as

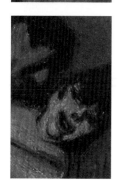

Frenzy

1900
pastel, 47.5 x 38.5 cm
private collection

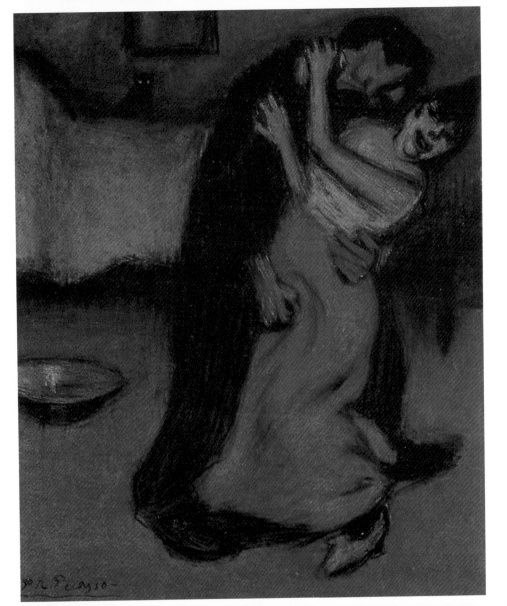

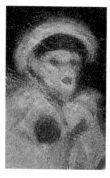

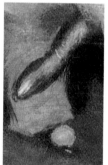

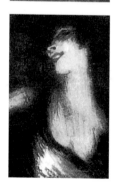

"fanatically autobiographical". That is the same as saying that he depended only on himself, on his *Erlebnis*. He was always free, owing nothing to anyone but himself." Indeed, everything convincingly shows that if Picasso depended on anything at all in his art, it was the constant need to express his inner state with the utmost fullness.

Pierrot and a Dancer

1900
oil on canvas, 38 x 46 cm
private collection

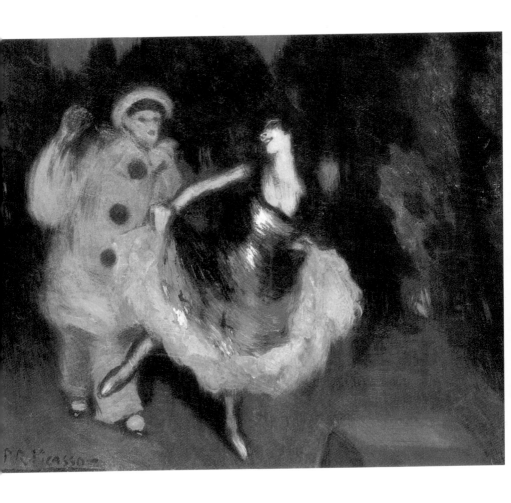

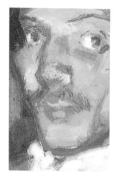

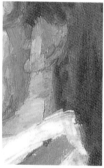

One may compare Picasso's œuvre with therapy; one may, as Kahnweiler did, regard Picasso as a Romantic artist. Let it also be noted that Picasso looked upon his art in a somewhat impersonal manner, took pleasure in the thought that the works, which he dated meticulously and helped scholars to catalogue, could serve as material for some future science.

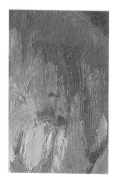

Self-Portrait

1901
oil on canvas, 73.5 x 60.5 cm
private collection

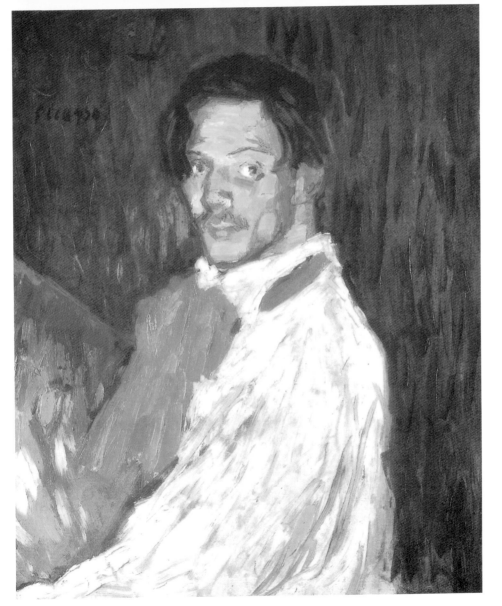

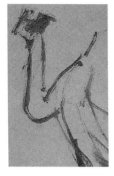

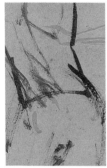

Kahnweiler testifies that in his old age Picasso spoke with greater approval of these early paintings than of those done in Barcelona, where the Ruiz Picasso family moved in the autumn of 1895 and where Pablo immediately enrolled as a student of painting in the School of Fine Arts called La Lonja.

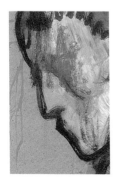

Two Figures in Profile
and the Head of a Man, Studies

1901
oil and tempera on paper, 41.2 x 57.2 cm
The Hermitage, St. Petersburg

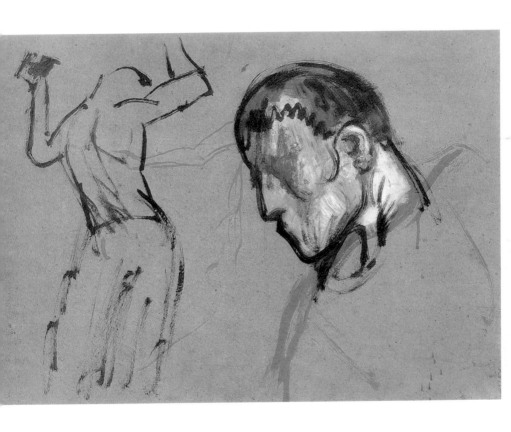

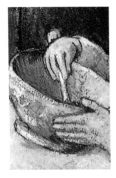

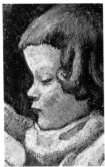

So as not to upset his father, Picasso spent two more years in there, during which time he could not but fall, albeit temporarily, under the deadening influence of academism, inculcated by the official school along with certain professional skills. "...I hate the period of my training at Barcelona," Picasso confessed to Kahnweiler.

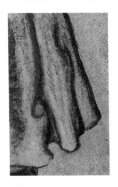

Le Gourmet
———————
1901
oil on canvas, 92.8 x 68.3 cm
The National Gallery, London

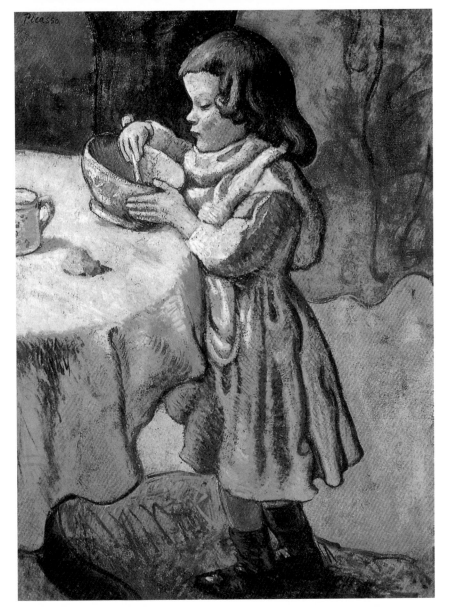

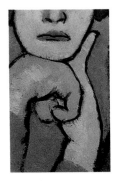

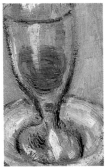

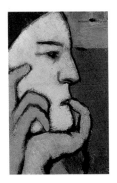

However, the studio which his father rented for him, and which gave him a certain freedom from both school and the stifling atmosphere of family relations, was a real support for his independence.

It was here that Picasso summarized the achievements of his school years by executing his first large canvases: *The First Communion* (winter of 1895-1896) and *Science and Charity* (beginning of 1897).

Harlequin and His Companion

1901
oil on canvas, 73 x 60 cm
The Pushkin Museum of Fine Arts, Moscow

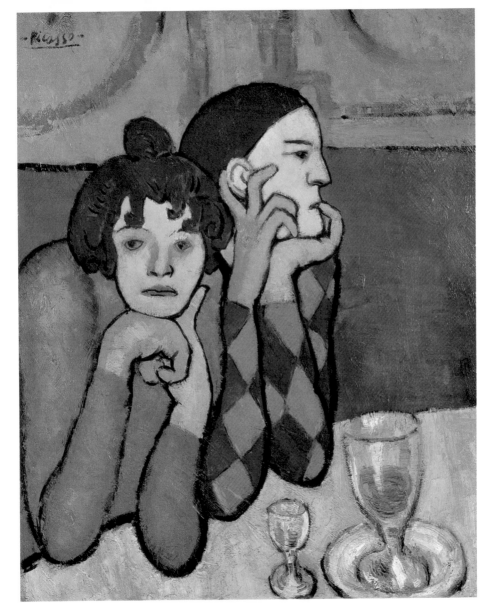

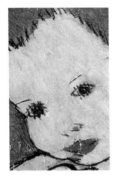

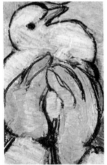

The latter received honourable mention at the national exhibition of fine arts in Madrid and was later awarded a gold medal at an exhibition in Málaga. His departure from home for Madrid in the autumn of 1897, supposedly to continue his formal education at the Royal Academy of San Fernando, in fact ushered in the period of post-study years – his years of wandering.

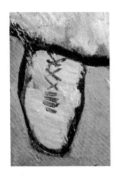

Child with a Pigeon

1901
oil on canvas, 73 x 54 cm
The National Gallery, London

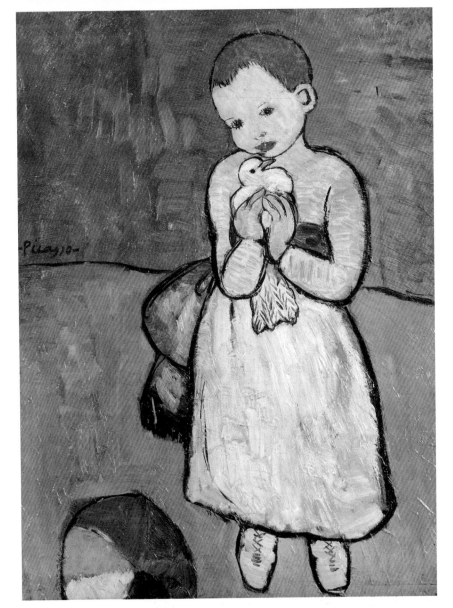

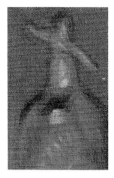

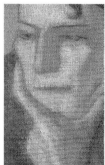

Pablo Picasso's wander-years consisted of several phases within a seven year period, from his initial departure to Madrid in 1897, to his final settling in Paris, artistic capital of the world, in the spring of 1904. To Picasso, Madrid meant first and foremost the Prado Museum, which he frequented more often than the Royal Academy of San Fernando in order to copy the Old Masters (he was particularly attracted by Velázquez).

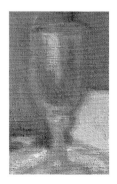

The Absinthe Drinker

1901
oil on canvas, 73 x 54 cm
The Hermitage, St. Petersburg

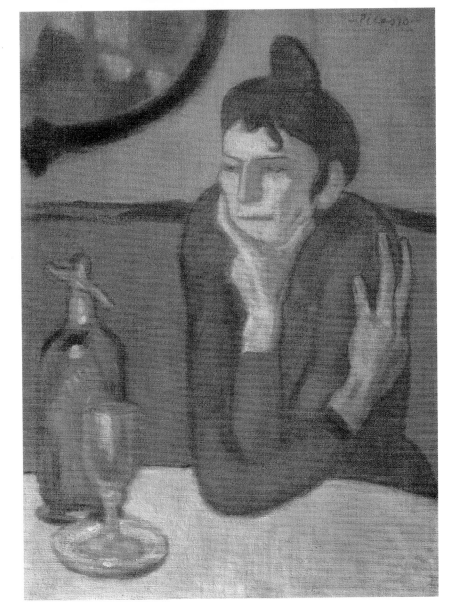

41

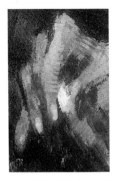

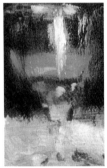

It might be said that the most important events for Picasso in the Spanish capital were the harsh winter of 1897-1898 and the subsequent illness that symbolically marked the end of his "academic career". In contrast, the time spent at Horta de Ebro – a village in the mountainous area of Catalonia, where he went to convalesce and where he remained for eight long months (until the spring of 1899) – was of such significance for Picasso that even decades later he would invariably repeat: "All that I know, I learnt in Horta de Ebro."

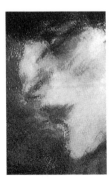

The Absinthe Drinker

1901
oil on cardboard, 65.5 x 50.8 cm
collection Mrs Melville Hall, New York

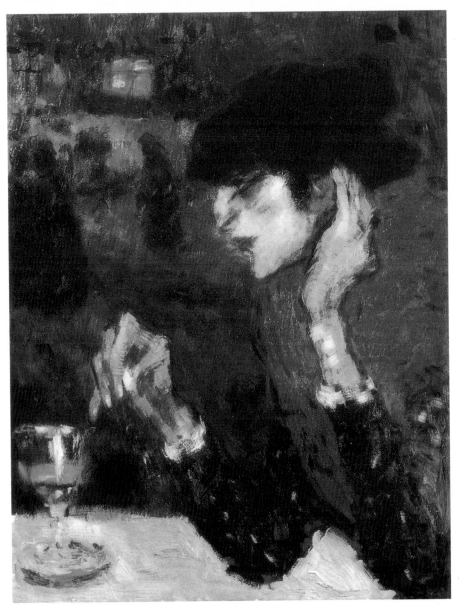

43

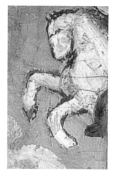

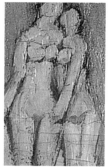

The months spent in this village were significant not so much in the sense of artistic production as for their key role in the young Picasso's creative biography, with its long process of maturation.

After his first stay at Horta de Ebro, a matured and renewed Picasso returned to Barcelona, which he now saw in a new light: as a centre of progressive trends, as a city open to modern ideas.

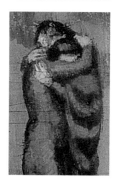

The Burial of Casagémas

1901
oil on wood, 146 x 89 cm
Musée du Petit Palais, Paris

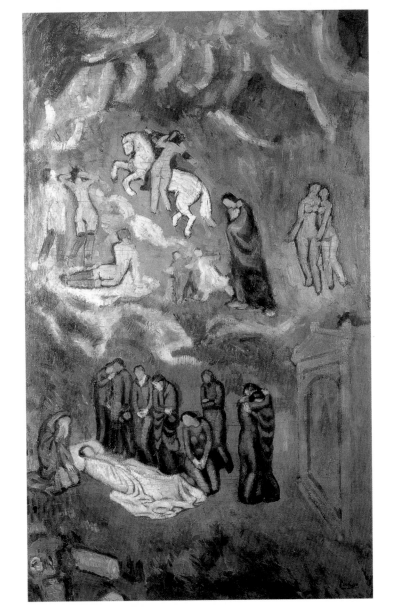

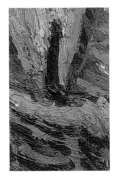

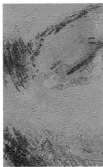

Indeed, Barcelona's modernism served to give the young Picasso an avant-garde education and to liberate his artistic thinking from classroom clichés. But this avant-garde universe was also merely the arena for his coming-to-be. Picasso, who in 1906 compared himself with a tenor who reaches a note higher than the one written in the score, was never the slave of what attracted him; in fact, Picasso invariably begins where influence ends.

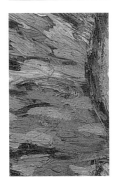

The Burial of Casagémas (Evocation)

1901
oil on canvas, 27 x 35 cm
Musée Picasso, Paris

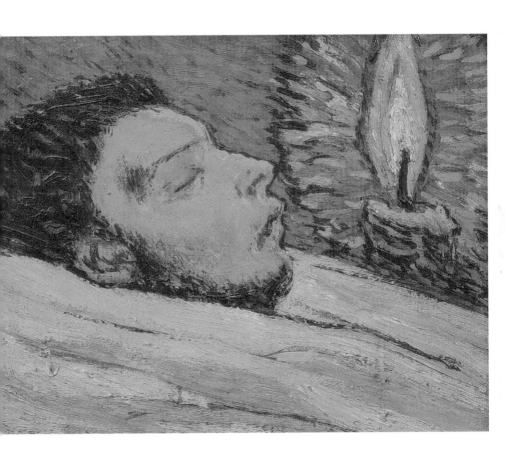

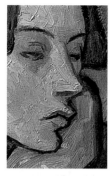

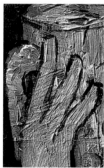

During those Barcelona years, as if caught up in a frenzy of graphic inspiration, Picasso drew a wealth of caricature portraits of his avant-garde friends.

During 1899 and 1900 the only subjects Picasso deemed worthy of painting were those which reflected the "final truth": the transience of human life and the inevitability of death.

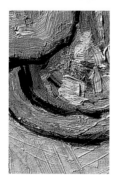

Portrait of the Poet Sabartes
(The Glass of Beer)

1901
oil on canvas, 82 x 66 cm
The Pushkin Museum of Fine Arts, Moscow

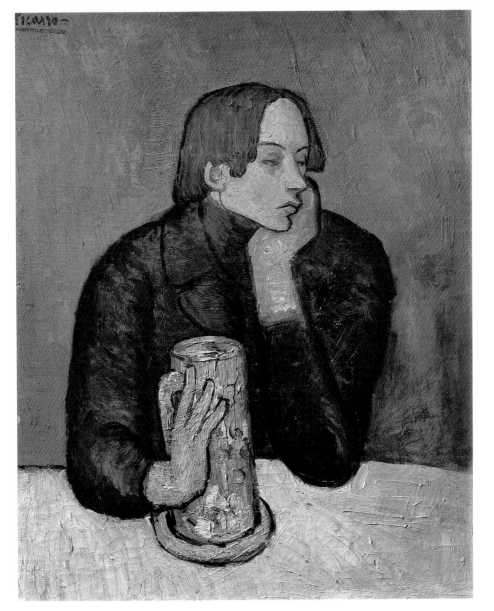

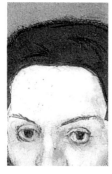

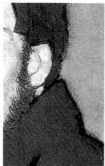

Bidding the deceased farewell, a vigil by the coffin, a cripple's agony on a hospital bed, a scene in a "death room" or near a dying woman's bed. Finally he executed a large composition called *The Last Moments*, which was shown in Barcelona at the beginning of 1900 and later that same year in Paris at the Exposition Universelle.

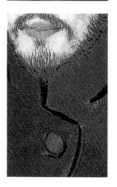

Self-Portrait

1901
oil on canvas, 81 x 60 cm
Musée Picasso, Paris

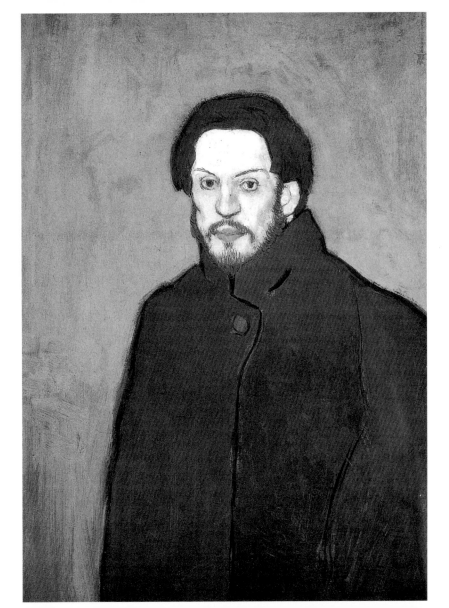

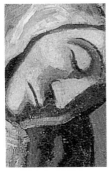

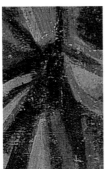

Picasso then re-used the canvas for his famous Blue Period painting *Life* (the earlier work was only recently discovered thanks to X-ray examination). He passed too rapidly through modernism and, having exhausted it, found himself at a dead-end, without a future.

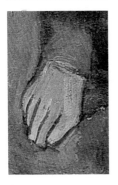

The Visit (Two Sisters)

1902
oil on wood, 152 x 100 cm
The Hermitage, St. Petersburg

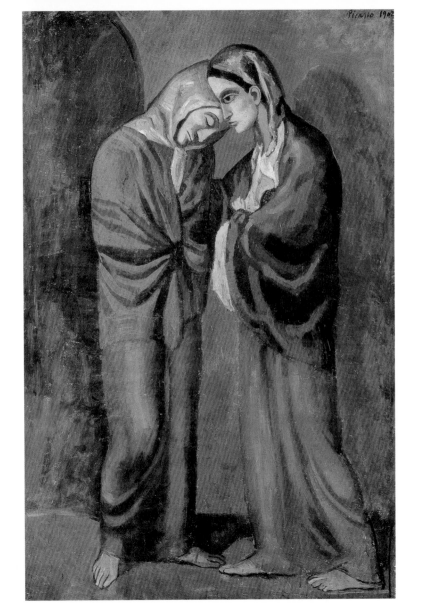

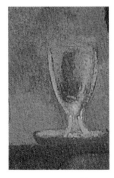

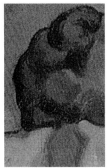

It was Paris that saved him, and after only two seasons there he wrote to his French friend Max Jacob in the summer of 1902 about how isolated he had felt in Barcelona among his friends who wrote "very bad books" and painted "idiotic pictures". Picasso arrived in Paris in October 1900. He moved into a studio in Montmartre, where he remained until the end of the year.

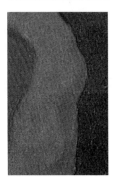

Prostitutes at the Bar

1902
oil on canvas, 80 x 91.4 cm
Hiroshima Museum of Art, Hiroshima

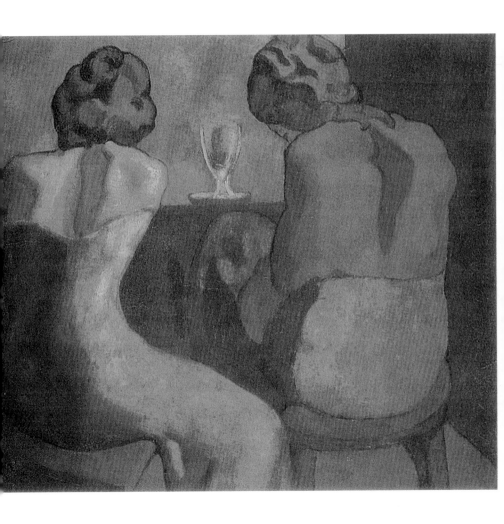

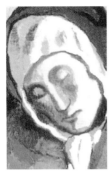

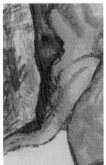

Although his contacts were limited to the Spanish colony, and even though he involuntarily looked at his surroundings with the eyes of a highly curious foreigner, Picasso immediately and without hesitation found his subject, becoming a painter of Montmartre. A joint letter by Picasso and his inseparable friend, the artist and poet Carlos Casagemas, bears the date of his nineteenth birthday (25 October 1900).

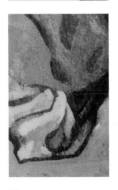

Poverty-Stricken Woman

1902
oil on canvas, 101.2 x 66 cm
Hiroshima Museum of Art, Hiroshima

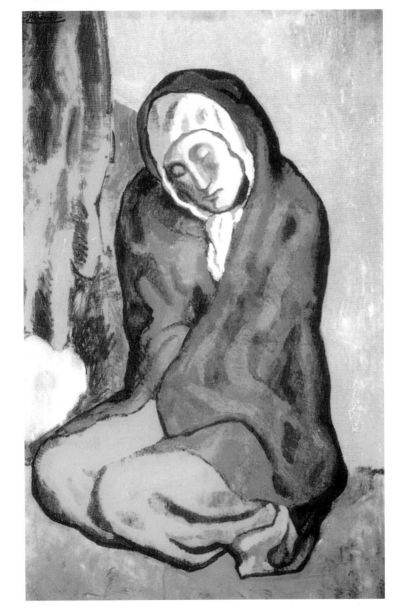

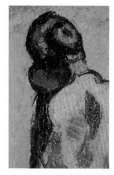

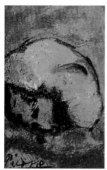

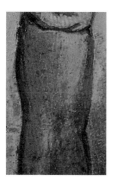

Written a few days after Pablo's arrival in Paris, it records their Parisian life; the pair inform a friend in Barcelona of their intensive work, of their intention to exhibit paintings at the Salon and in Spain, of their going to café-concerts and theatres in the evening; they describe their new acquaintances, their leisure activities, their studio. The letter exudes high spirits and reflects their intoxicating delight with life: "If you see Opisso, tell him to come, since it's good for saving the soul – tell him to send Gaudí and the Sagrada Familia to hell... Here there are real teachers everywhere."

Mother and Child

1902
oil on canvas, 40.5 x 33 cm
Scottish National Gallery of Modern Art, Edinburgh

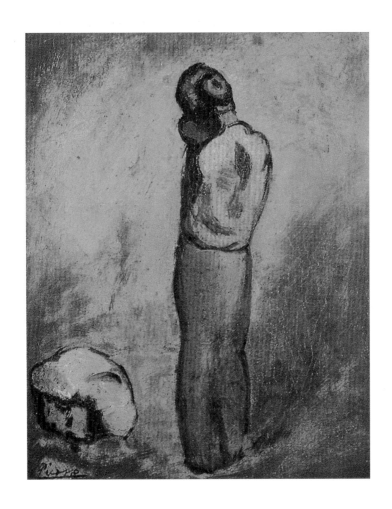

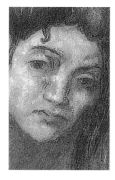

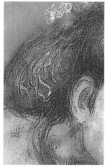

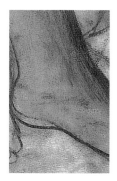

Vast exhibition halls of paintings at the Exposition Universelle (number 79 in the Spanish section was: Pablo Ruiz Picasso, *Les Derniers Moments*), the retrospective Centennale and Décennale de l'Art Français, great shows with paintings by Ingres and Delacroix, Courbet and the Impressionists, up to and including Cézanne; the gigantic Louvre with its endless halls of masterpieces and sculptures of ancient civilizations; whole streets of galleries and shops showing and dealing in new-style painting...

Nude Woman with Crossed Legs

1903
pastel, 58 x 44 cm
private collection

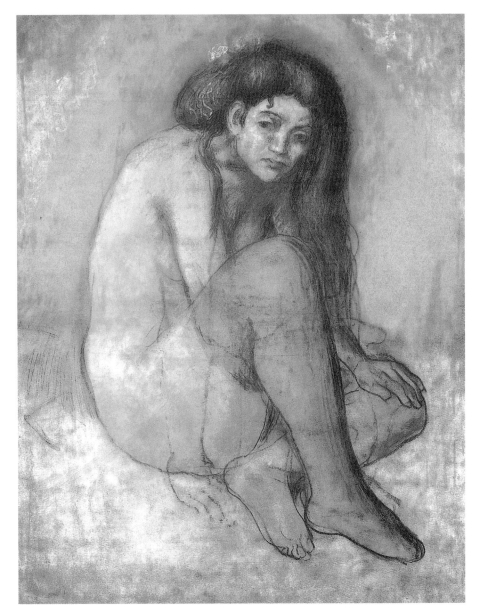

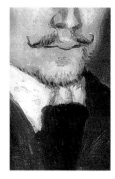

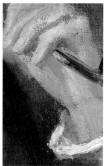

He was staggered by the abundance of artistic impressions, by this new feeling of freedom.

Picasso's "real teachers" were nonetheless the older painters of Montmartre, who helped him discover the broad spectrum of local subject matter: the popular dances, the café-concerts with their stars, the attractive and sinister world of nocturnal joys, electrified by the glow of feminine charms, but also the everyday melancholy and nostalgic atmosphere of small streets on the city outskirts.

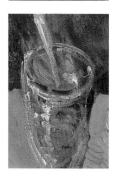

Portrait of Soler

1903
oil on canvas, 100 x 70 cm
The Hermitage, St. Petersburg

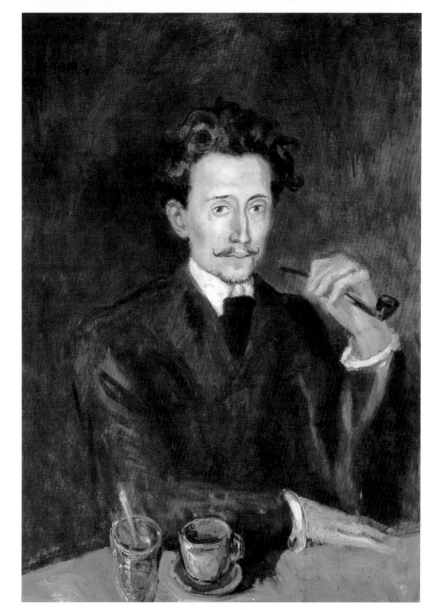

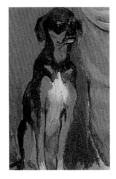

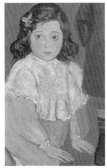

Picasso entered then his so-called Cabaret Period. This subject matter attracted him because it afforded the possibility to express the view that life is a drama and that its heart is the sexual urge. And yet the direct, expressive and austerely realistic treatment of these subjects reminds one not so much of French influences as of Goya's late period.

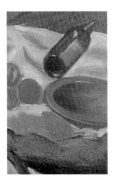

The Soler Family
_____

1903
oil on canvas, 150 x 200 cm
Musée d'Art Moderne et d'Art Contemporain, Liège

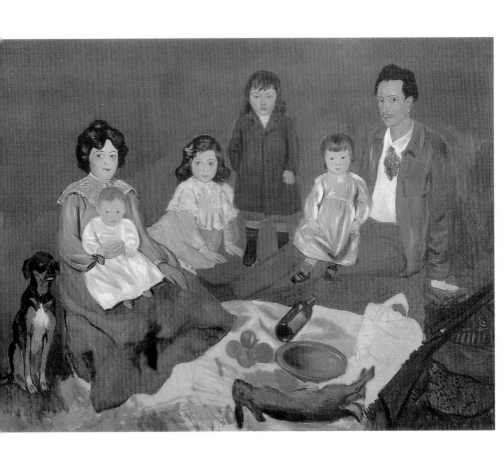

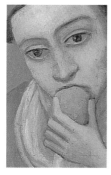

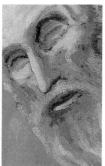

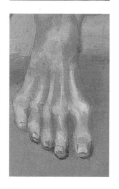

The artist's sudden departure from Paris in December 1900 looks like a flight. His friend Casagemas shot himself in a café on the Boulevard de Clichy, after returning to Paris despite Picasso's attempts to help him find a measure of peace under the Spanish sun.

Back in Madrid, Picasso undertook the publication of a magazine called *Arte Joven (Young Art)*.

Old Jew and a Boy

1903
oil on canvas, 125 x 92 cm
The Pushkin Museum of Fine Arts, Moscow

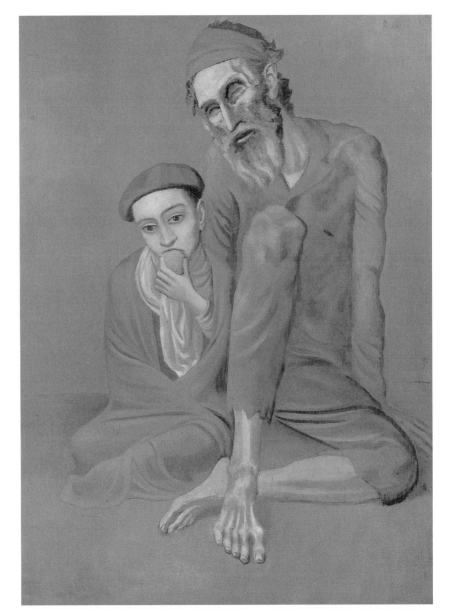

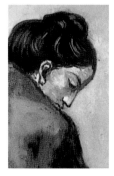

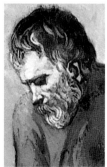

He also painted society scenes and female portraits. Daix believes that Casagemas's suicide was no small influence. This short "Society" Period (to a certain extent, a young artist's reaction to the temptations of public recognition) ran itself out by the spring of 1901 when, after a stay in Barcelona, Picasso returned to Paris. An exhibition of his works was planned in the gallery of the well-known dealer Ambroise Vollard.

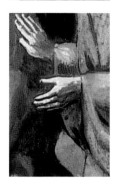

Poor People on the Seashore (The Tragedy)

1903
oil on wood, 105.4 x 69 cm
National Gallery of Art Chester Dale Collection
Washington

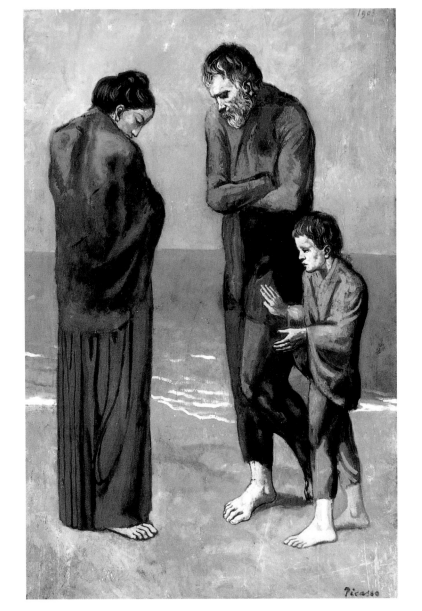

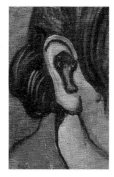

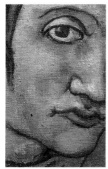

Throughout May and the first half of June 1901, Picasso worked very hard, on some days producing two or even three paintings. He "had begun where he had broken off six months before." He used the Impressionist freedom of sinuous brushstrokes, the Japanese precision of Degas's compositions and Toulouse-Lautrec's posters, the heightened, exalted vividness of Van Gogh's colours, heralding the coming of Fauvism, which manifested itself fully only in 1905.

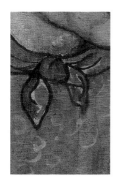

Head of a Woman with a Scarf

1903
oil on canvas, pasted on cardboard, 50 x 36.5 cm
The Hermitage, St. Petersburg

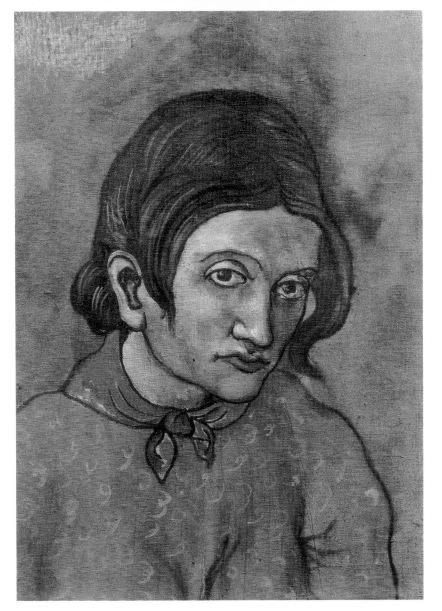

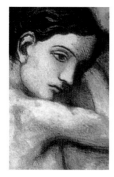

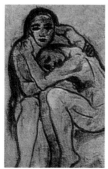

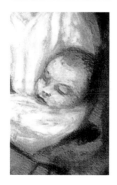

But Picasso's so-called pre-Fauvism of the spring of 1901 was of a purely aesthetic, rather than of a subjective, psychological nature.

Picasso exhibited over sixty-five paintings and drawings at the Vollard exhibition that opened on 24 June. Some had been brought from Spain, but the overwhelming majority were done in Paris.

Life
———
1903
oil on canvas, 196.5 x 128.5 cm
The Cleveland Museum of Art, Cleveland

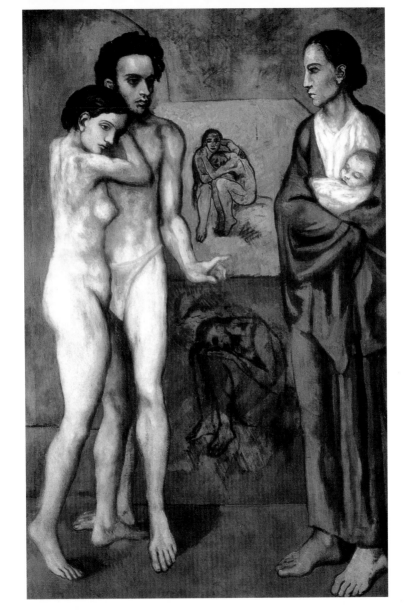

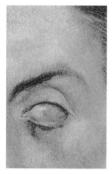

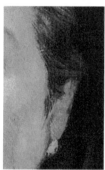

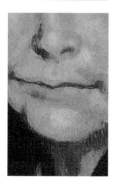

Jarring, often shocking subjects, spontaneous, insistent brushwork, nervous, frenzied colours typify the so-called Vollard style. But even though the exhibition was a financial success, many of the pre-Fauve Vollard-style paintings would be painted over in the very near future.

Celestina

1904
oil on canvas, 81 x 60 cm
Musée Picasso, Paris

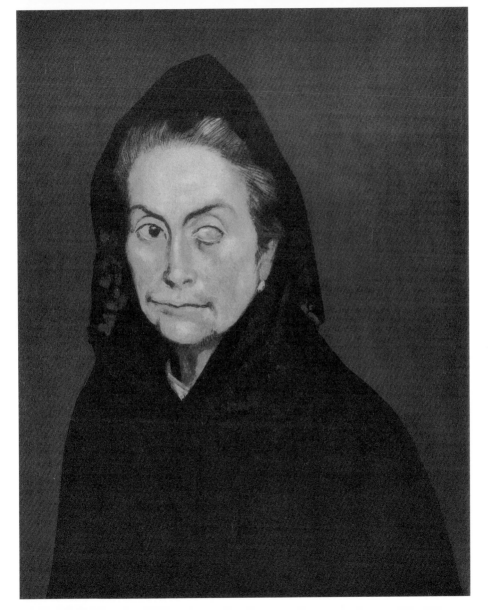

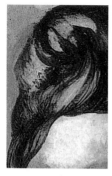

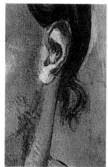

Two canvases dating from this period, *Harlequin and His Companion* and *The Absinthe Drinker*, deal with one of the early Picasso's favourite subjects: people in cafés. From the viewpoint of style they are sometimes characterized as examples of the so-called Stained-Glass Period (because of the powerful, flexible dark line dividing the major colour planes, typical of work of that period).

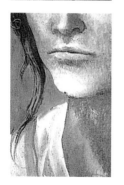

Woman with a Helmet of Hair (An Acrobat's Wife)

1904
gouache on cardboard, 42.8 x 31 cm
The Art Institute of Chicago, Chicago

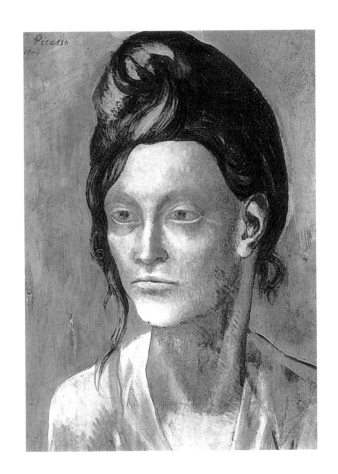

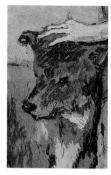

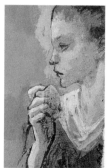

This style of painting had close aesthetic ties with the Art Nouveau (it derives from Gauguin's Cloisonnism and the arabesques of Toulouse-Lautrec's posters-styles Picasso rated highly at that time); here, however, it is a poetic testament to the predominance of the intellectual principle in Picasso's work.

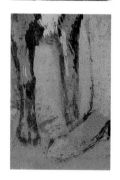

Boy with a Dog

―――――――――――

1905
gouache on cardboard, 57.2 x 41.2 cm
The Hermitage, St. Petersburg

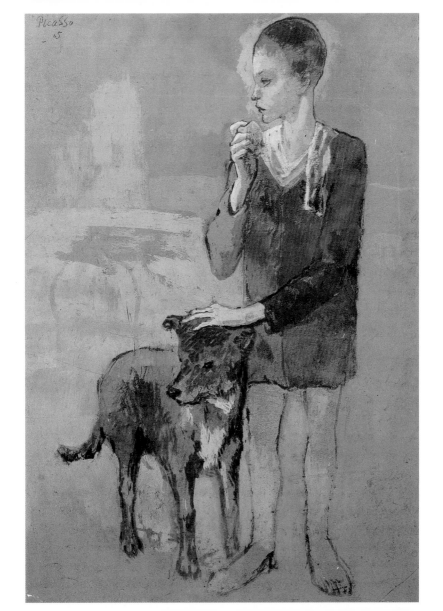

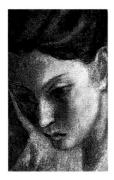

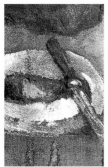

In formal terms, *Harlequin and His Companion* and *The Absinthe Drinker* continue Gauguin's line, but emotionally and ideologically, they follow Van Gogh, who perceived his *Night Café* as a horrible place, "a place where one can perish, go insane, commit a crime."

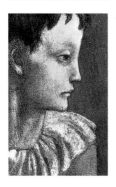

Tumblers (Mother and Son)

1905
gouache on canvas, 90 x 71 cm
Staatsgalerie, Stuttgart

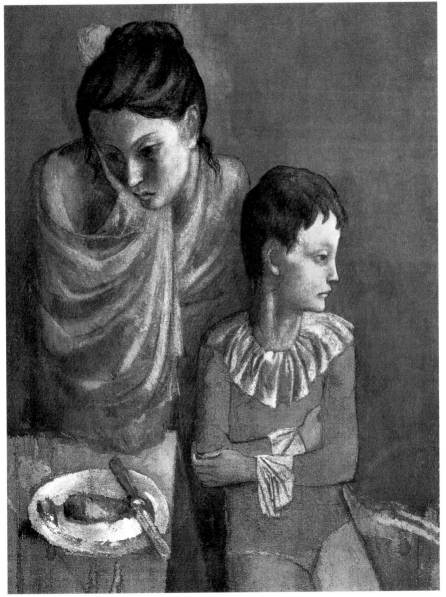

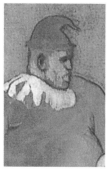

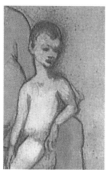

Generally speaking, one sees here the predominance of form in the composition and the sentimental themes that Daix defined as two of the three essentials of the new style ripening in Picasso throughout the second half of 1901. The third – the use of monochromatic blue – gave this new style its name: the Blue Period. It came into its own late in 1901 and lasted until the end of 1904.

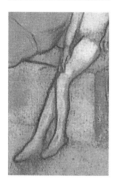

Clown with a Young Acrobat
─────────────────────────

1905
charcoal, pastel and water-colours on paper, 60 x 47 cm
Göteborg Konstmuseum, Göteborg

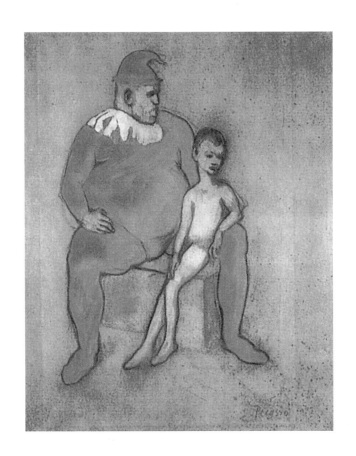

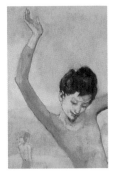

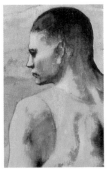

Even though Picasso himself repeatedly insisted on the inner, subjective nature of the Blue Period, its genesis and, especially, the monochromatic blue were for many years explained as merely the results of various aesthetic influences. When, however, after sixty-five years of obscurity, the paintings inspired by the death of his friend Casagemas in the autumn of 1901 saw the light of day, the psychological motive behind the Blue Period seemed to have been discovered.

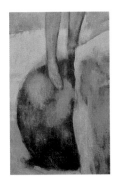

Young Acrobat on a Ball

1905
oil on canvas, 147 x 95 cm
The Pushkin Museum of Fine Arts, Moscow

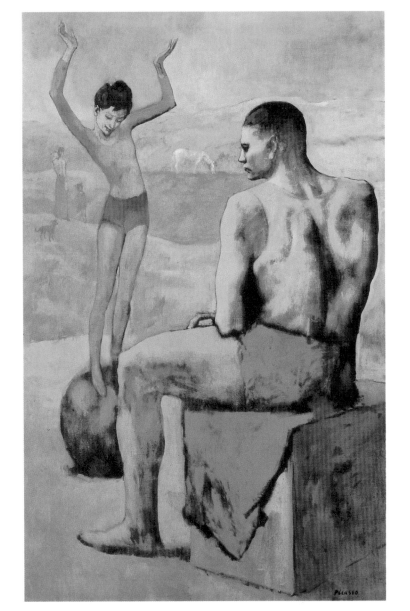

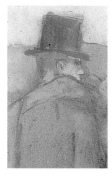

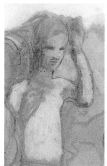

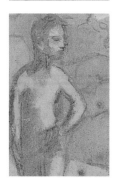

"It was when thinking that Casagemas was dead that I began to paint in blue," Picasso told Daix. Blue is cold, it is the colour of sorrow, grief, misfortune, inner pain; but blue is also the most spiritual of colours, the colour of space, thoughts and dreams that know no confines. In one of his poems of the 1900s Picasso wrote, "You are the best of what exists in the world. The colour of all colours… the most blue of all the blues."

Family of Saltimbanques (Comedians)

1905
gouache and charcoal on cardboard, 51.2 x 61.2 cm
The Hermitage, St. Petersburg

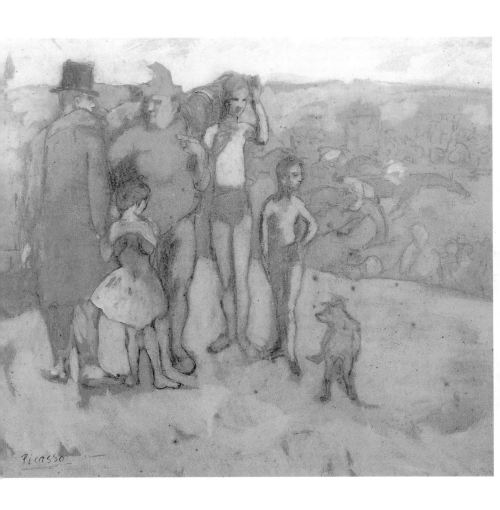

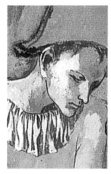

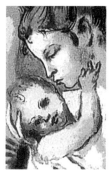

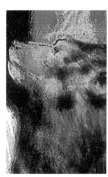

The Blue Period as a whole, throughout its entire three years, resulted in an art that was heterogeneous and complex, not only in style but also in content.

The *Portrait of the Poet Sabartés,* according to Sabartés himself, belongs to the time of the Blue Period's inception; it was created in Paris in October-November 1901.

Family of Acrobats with a Monkey

_____

1905
gouache water-colours
pastel and Chinese ink on cardboard 104 x 75 cm
Göteborg Konstmuseum, Göteborg

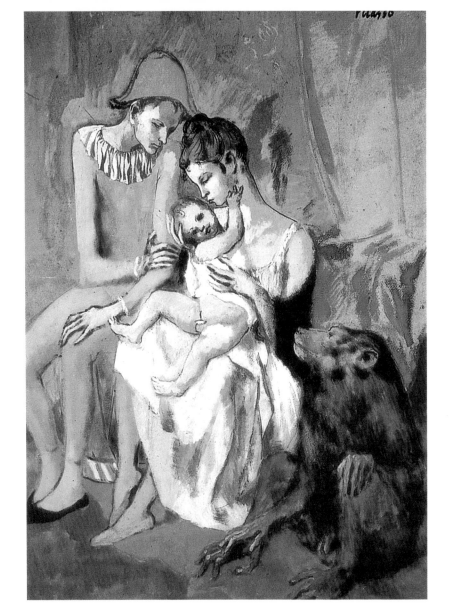

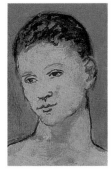

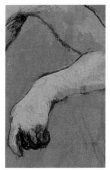

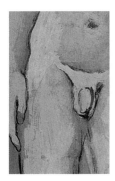

Blue is the picture's actual subject, an expression of the state of mind of the poet. The blue colour is abstract and universal, it makes Sabartés figure, seated at a café table, a symbol of poetic melancholy that looms over the world's empty horizon.

Blue is the painting's metaphor for sadness and sorrow; however, towards the end of 1901, the desire to express these feelings more directly motivated Picasso to turn to sculpture.

Naked Boy
———
1905
tempera on cardboard, 67.5 x 52 cm
The Hermitage, St. Petersburg

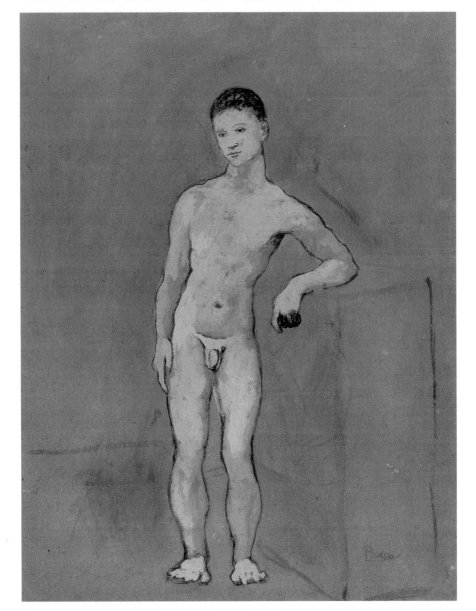

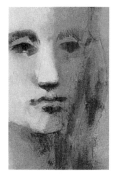

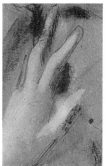

The predominance of form in his paintings, mentioned by Daix, undeniably testifies to this interest; Picasso began to sculpt not only because the medium made his plastic idea more concrete, but also because it corresponded to his need to impose strict limits on himself, to achieve the most ascetic means of expression.

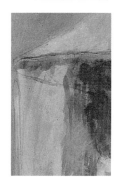

Spanish Woman from Majorca

1905
gouache and watercolour on cardboard, 67 x 51 cm
The Pushkin Museum of Fine Arts, Moscow

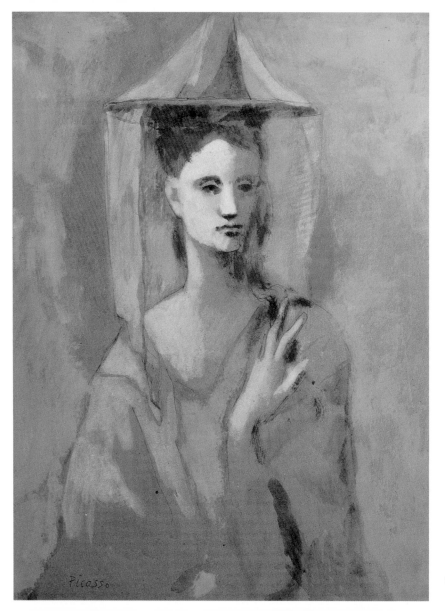

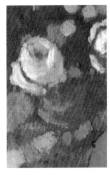

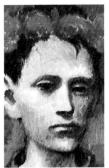

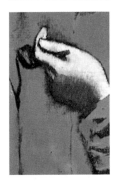

In the painting *The Visit*, everything pertaining to the depicted event is generalized and frugal. Picasso not only cut back on details, he consciously limited his means of expression to the point of asceticism. The indistinct and simple monochromatic blue corresponds to the composition's elemental quality, the generalized plastic and linear character.

Boy with a Pipe
———————————
1905
oil on canvas, 100 x 81.3 cm
Mrs John Hay Whitney Collection, New York

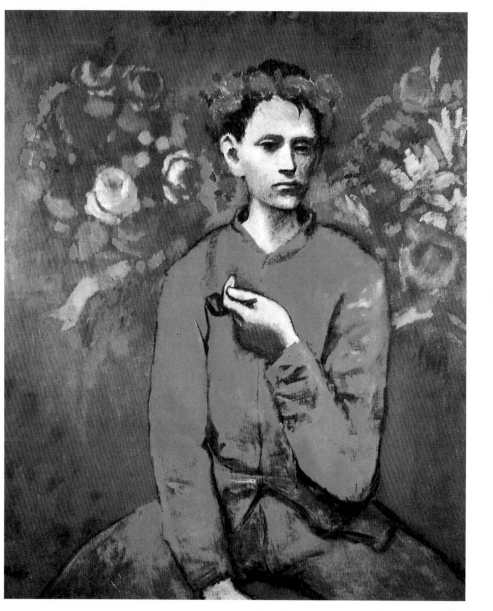

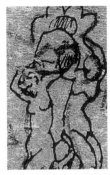

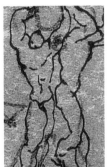

While simplifying the form, Picasso gave the content greater complexity and depth, turning the initial subject into a timeless, universal event – the mournful meeting of two symbolic sisters in another world. It may well be that in *The Visit* Picasso first discovered for himself the law of the associative and plastic equation of different objects.

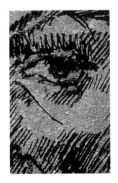

Head of an Old Man with a Crown

1905
paper, pen, Indian ink, pastel, 17 x 10 cm
The Pushkin Museum of Fine Arts, Moscow

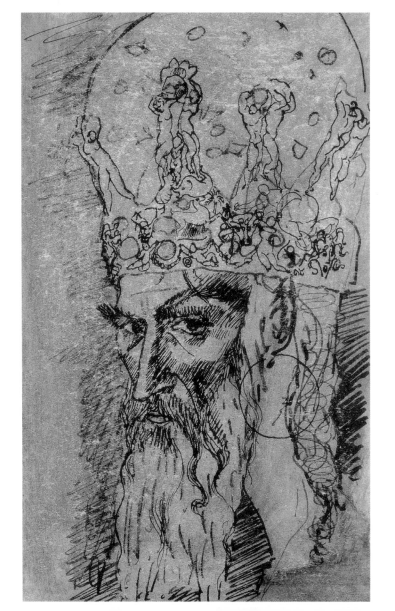

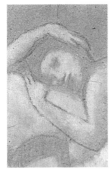

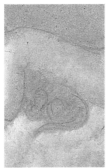

It would later become an active and important instrument of his poetic imagery, the poetry of metamorphosis, born during the Cubist Period and preserved to the very end. *The Visit*, probably completed by the autumn of 1902, is the culmination of the first phase of the Blue Period.

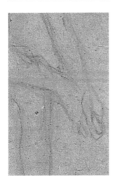

Interior Scene: Nude Woman beside a Cat and a Nude Man

1905
Gouache, charcoal on cardboard, 52 x 67.5 cm
The Hermitage, St. Petersburg

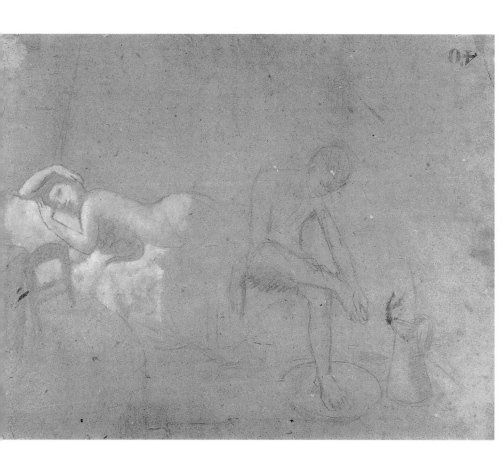

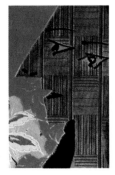

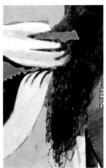

During 1902, three quarters of which Picasso spent in Barcelona, his art strayed far from reality into the area of transcendent ideas expressing only his subjective, spiritual experience. His characters were vague, anonymous, timeless. These are images of ideas. Their visual definition dealing with the plastic modelling of simple forms, the feeling for volume and broad linear rhythms are more typical of a sculptor than of the inspiration of a painter.

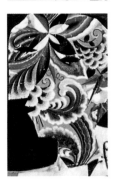

La Toilette

1906
oil on canvas
Albright-Knox Art Gallery Buffalo, New York

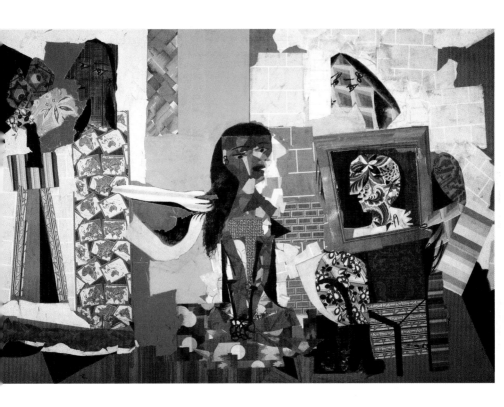

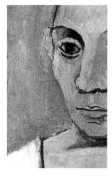

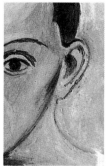

This was a time when Picasso, as Daix noted, wished to achieve the *mélange* of form and idea. The fact that Picasso turned to his first friend in Paris, the poet Max Jacob, for understanding at least in part explains his return in October 1902 to Paris. There they lived in poverty together and after having suffered for three months from cold weather and misery, Picasso left in mid-January 1903.

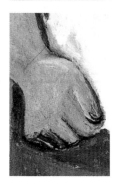

Self-Portrait with a Palette

1906
oil on canvas, 92 x 73 cm
Philadelphia Museum of Art, Philadelphia

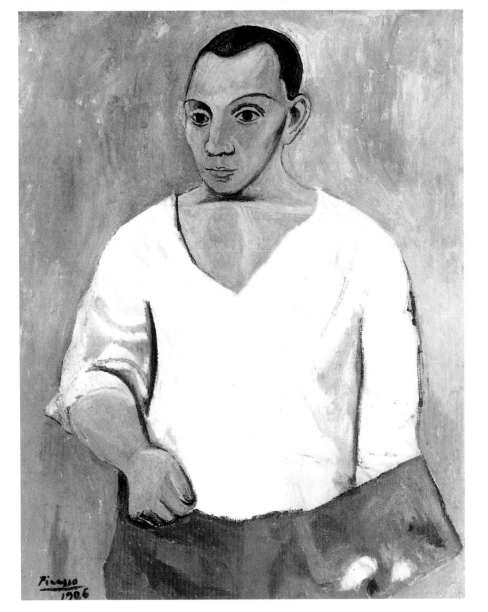

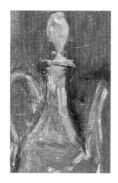

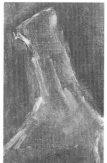

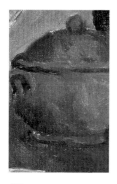

Yet, as with previous trips, this visit to Paris introduced something new to his art.

Not having the means to paint in oil in Paris, Picasso made drawings; thus, when he resumed painting in Barcelona, his new graphic experience manifested itself in his greater attention to the problems of space, of human anatomy, of the tangible features of his characters.

Glassware, Still-Life with a Porro

1906
oil on canvas, 38.4 x 56 cm
The Hermitage, St. Petersburg

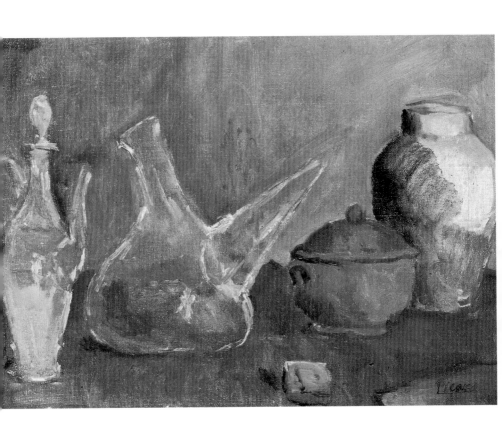

105

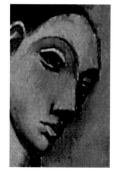

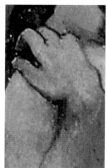

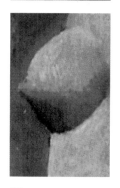

In the most significant works of the first half of 1903 – *Poor People on the Seashore (The Tragedy)*, *Life* and *The Embrace* – Picasso developed the universal Blue Period themes as scenes of relations between individualized characters.

For his consciousness sought a way out in the external, in reality. This urge for the concrete was expressed in cityscapes and especially in the portraiture which manifested itself in the middle of 1903.

Two Naked Women

1906
oil on canvas, 151.3 x 93 cm
The Museum of Modern Art, New York

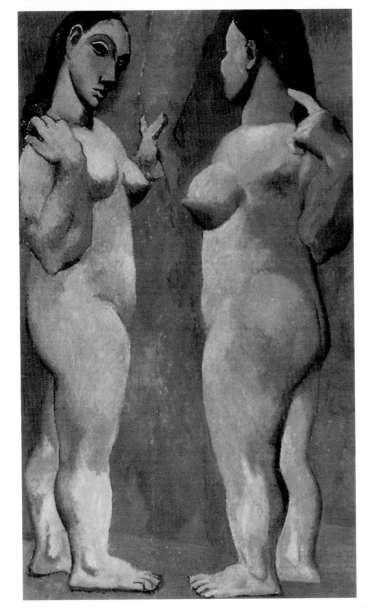

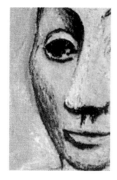

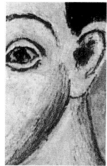

That was when the *Portrait of Soler* was created, following a portrait of Soler's wife and a group portrait of the entire family during a summer picnic: three canvases that work as a triptych. In the unquestionable masterpiece of the autumn of 1903, *Old Jew and a Boy,* the contact with external reality makes the theme of man's unhappiness concrete by dramatic images of poverty and physical infirmity.

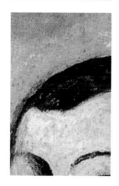

Self-Portrait

1906
oil on canvas, 65 x 54 cm
Musée Picasso, Paris

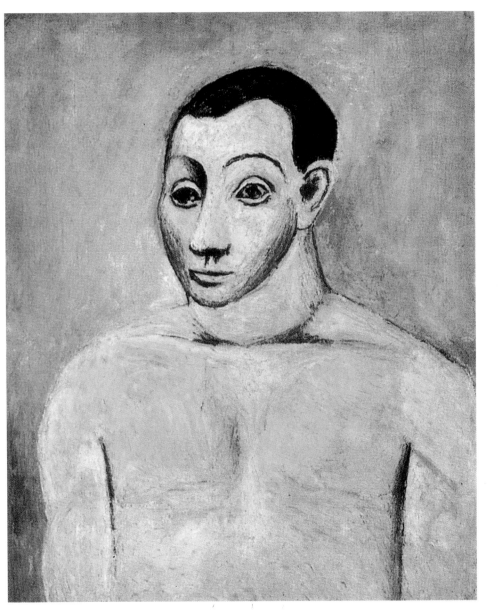

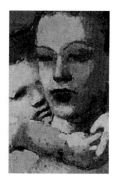

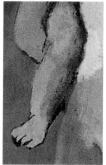

Among the paintings of the Blue Period, this is perhaps the most monochromatic and homogeneous in tonality. In *Old Jew and a Boy* the artist interprets the humanistic myth of the nineteenth century, but does it with a Biblical hopelessness for human fate. The painting shows us how Picasso's aesthetic crisis of the "blue years" was to be resolved.

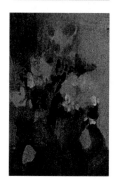

The Two Brothers

1906
gouache on cardboard, 80 x 59 cm
Musée Picasso, Paris

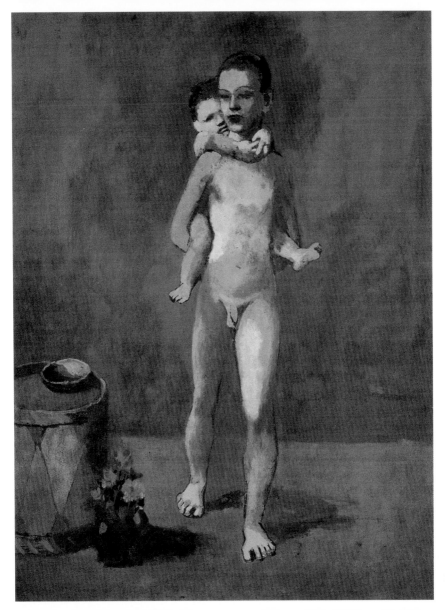

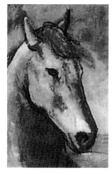

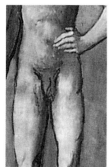

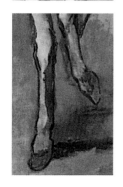

For here the striving to attain extreme expressiveness had necessitated the tangible interplay of lithe plastic forms, the complex linear rhythms, the mimetic contrasts of types, and, finally, the intensely ash-blue colour.

In 1904 the Blue Period, with its pessimistic, ingrown character and furious desire for an aesthetic absolute, reached its climax.

Boy Leading a Horse

1906
oil on canvas, 220.3 x 130.6 cm
The Museum of Modern Art, New York

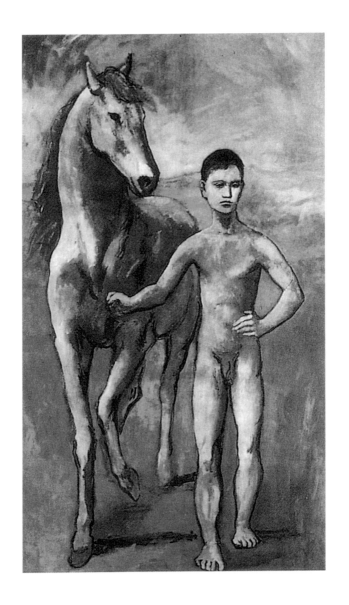

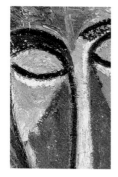

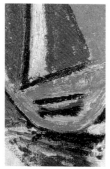

This crisis of youth had to be replaced by a new stage in the process of individual development – the stage of self-building. Not accidentally, Picasso now set stock by external conditions, planning another trip to Paris to breathe different air, speak another language, see other faces and adopt another lifestyle. In April 1904 he went back to Paris – for good, as it was to turn out.

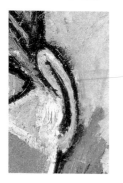

Nude (Half-Length)
_____

1907
oil on canvas, 61 x 47 cm
The Hermitage, St. Petersburg

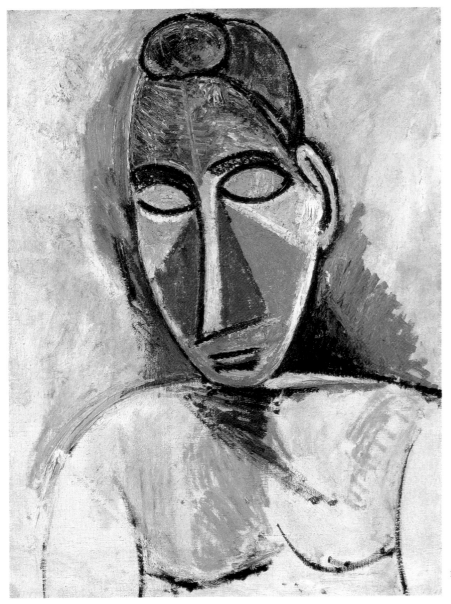

115

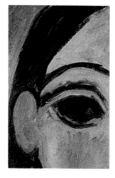

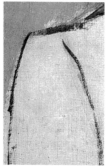

He moved into a studio building known as the Bateau-Lavoir (Laundry Barge), a nickname given to it by Max Jacob for its strange design. A dilapidated wooden house that clung to the heights of Montmartre, which was pastorally peaceful in those times, the Bateau-Lavoir became Picasso's home for the next five years, and the atmosphere of this bohemian nest, its texture of poverty, became the atmosphere and texture of his canvases of 1904-1908.

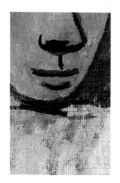

Chest of a Woman

1907
study for *Les Demoiselles d'Avignon*
oil on canvas, 47 x 59 cm
Musée Picasso, Paris

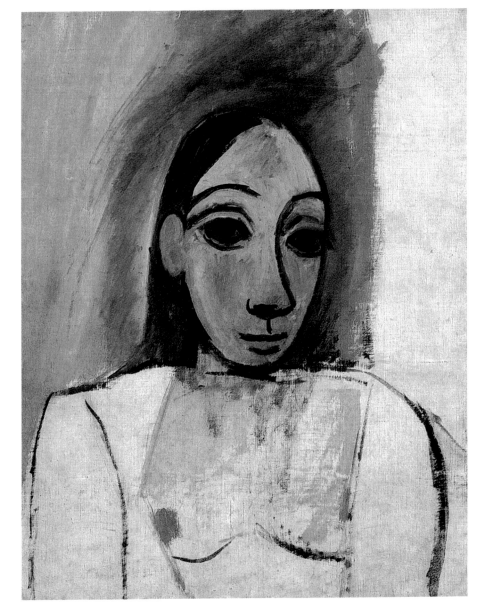

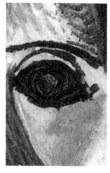

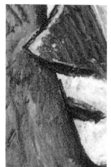

Picasso's life soon entered family waters, when he met and took up with the beautiful Fernande Olivier. Being with colleagues became less important to Picasso than meeting creative figures from other fields, especially poets, who included André Salmon and Guillaume Apollinaire.

Among Picasso's first Parisian friends were Suzanne Bloch, later a well-known singer, and her brother, the violinist Henri Bloch.

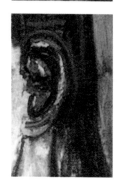

Chest of a Woman

1907
study for *Les Demoiselles d'Avignon*
oil on canvas, 65 x 58 cm
Centre Georges Pompidou, Paris

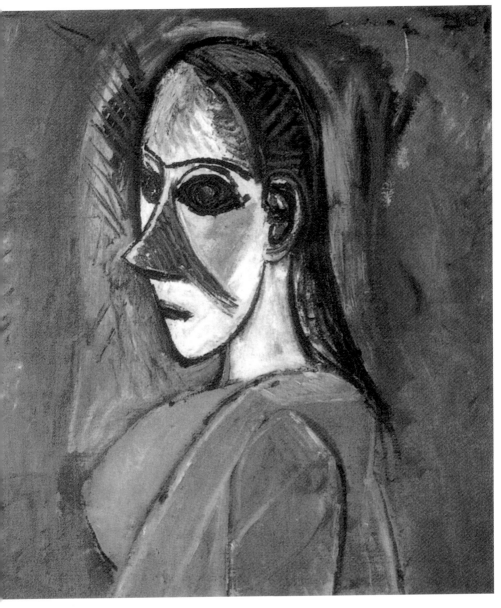

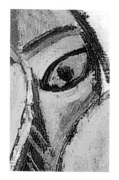

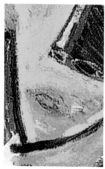

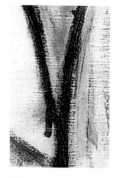

In 1904 he gave the couple a photo of himself, executed a brilliant portrait of Suzanne, and presented Henri Bloch with a small canvas, *Head of a Woman with a Scarf*.

This work, usually dated to 1903, when Picasso was in Barcelona, is nevertheless more typical of his first Parisian months of 1904, when he used watercolours extensively and worked in the graphic arts.

Head

———

1907
study for *Les Demoiselles d'Avignon*
oil on canvas, 96 x 33 cm
Kunstmuseum, Basel

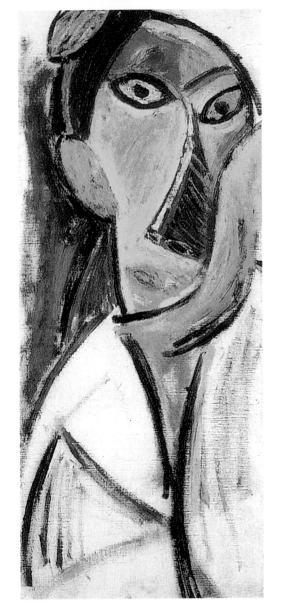

121

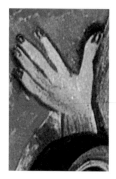

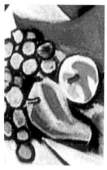

The blue has now been diluted, it is nearly translucent and has red undertones; the drawing is strong and combines attention to detail with expressive stylization. At the same time (and this is characteristic of the end of the Blue Period), the source of the mood is now the individual psychology of the character.

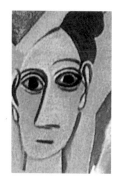

Les Demoiselles d'Avignon

1907
oil on canvas, 243.9 x 233.7 cm
The Museum of Modern Art, New York

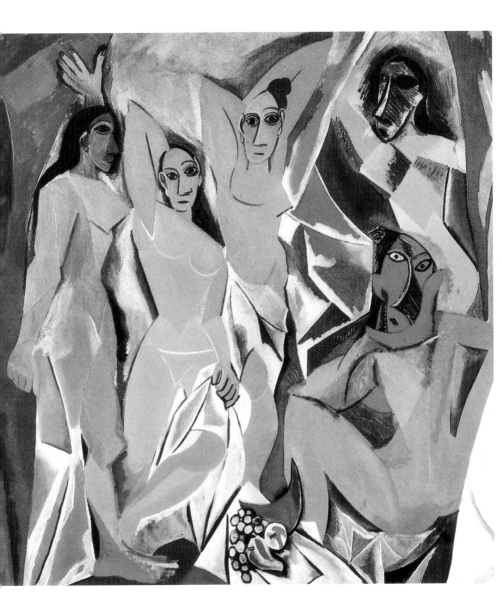

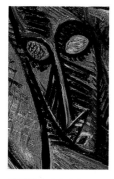

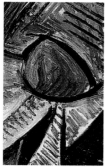

The themes began to come from the world of travelling circuses. Picasso perceived the world of the travelling circus as a metaphor for his own environment – the artistic Bohemia of Montmartre, which lived "poorly, but splendidly" (Max Jacob) in feverish excitement and hunger-sharpened sensitivity, in the brotherhood of companionable joviality and the wrenching melancholy of alienation.

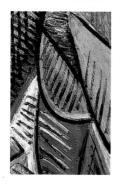

The Dance of the Veils (Nude with Draper)

1907
oil on canvas, 150 x 100 cm
The Hermitage, St. Petersburg

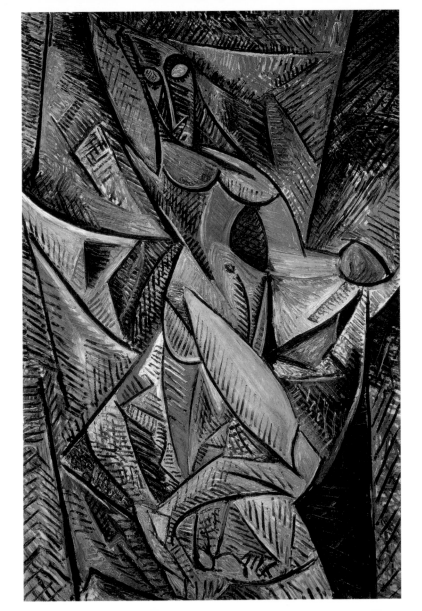

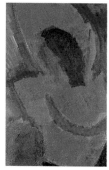

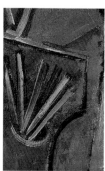

This mood of calm, sentimental melancholy was the leitmotif of Picasso's works from late 1904 and the first half of 1905, the so-called Circus or Rose Period.

And all the works of that period, including the gouache *Boy with a Dog*, are related, some more, some less, to the huge composition on the life of a travelling circus that the artist envisioned at the end of 1904.

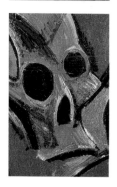

Composition with a Skull

1907
oil on canvas, 115 x 88 cm
The Hermitage, St. Petersburg

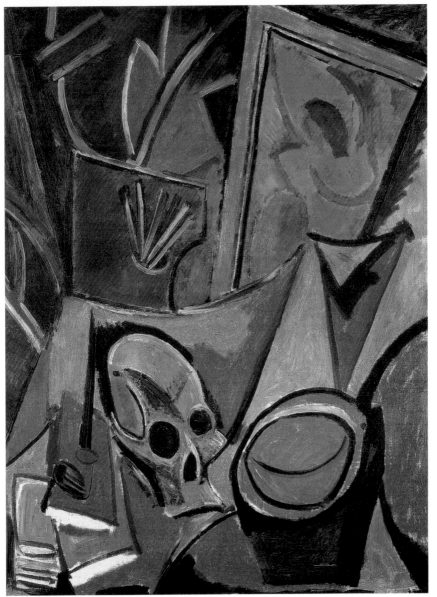

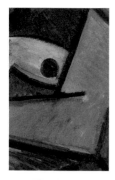

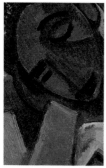

The chief products of the Circus Period, sometimes also called the Saltimbanque Period, was the *Family of Saltimbanques* created towards the end of 1905. Recent laboratory studies reveal the complex evolution of the painting in both concept and composition. The central motif of the original composition was preserved and rethought in the famous painting *Girl on a Ball*.

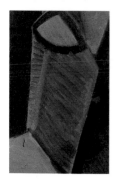

Woman Seated (Nude Woman Seated)

1907-1908
oil on canvas, 150 x 99 cm
The Hermitage, St. Petersburg

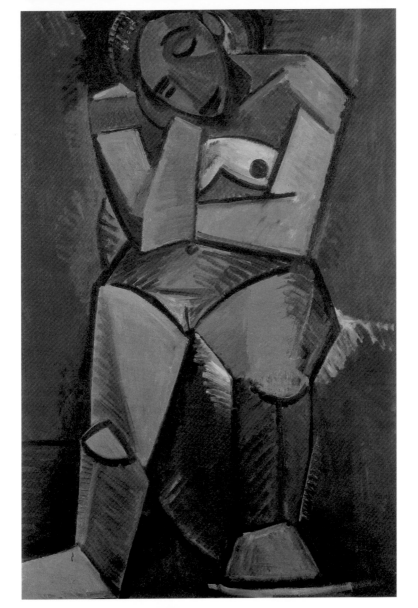

129

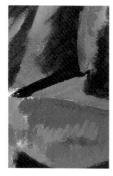

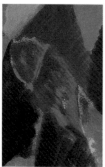

Girl on a Ball was painted only a few months after its source, *Saltimbanques*, and serves as a kind of answer by Picasso to Gauguin's question: *"Where Do We Come from? What Are We? Where Are We Going?"*

Picasso's original intention was still quite literary. But if, in this painting from the first half of 1905, the issue of form is still in its genesis, its magnitude, complexity and potential can already be sensed.

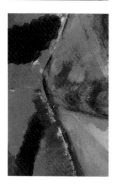

Friendship

1908
oil on canavs, 152 x 101 cm
The Hermitage, St. Petersburg

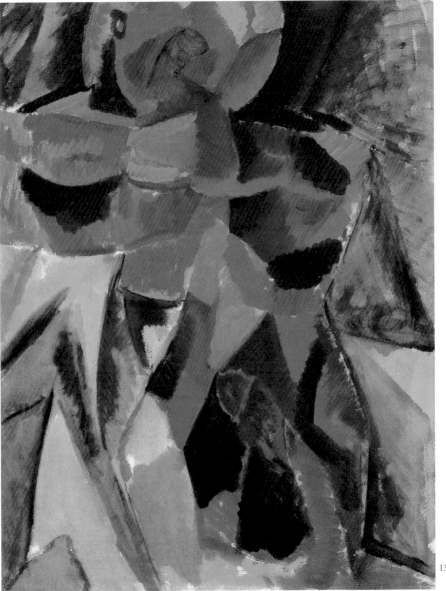

131

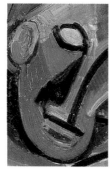

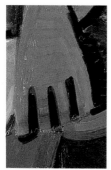

That is why the *Girl on a Ball* stands out among Picasso's creations as the seed of many further developments in the area of plastic form and imagery.

The hieratically mysterious figures of the autumn of 1905 (*Spanish Woman from Majorca*) were to disappear from his art, while the persistent preoccupation with sources led him to the theme of primal nudity and youthfulness.

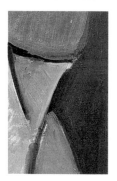

Friendship

1908
sketch, watercolour and gouache on paper, 61.9 x 47.6 cm
The Pushkin Museum of Fine Arts, Moscow

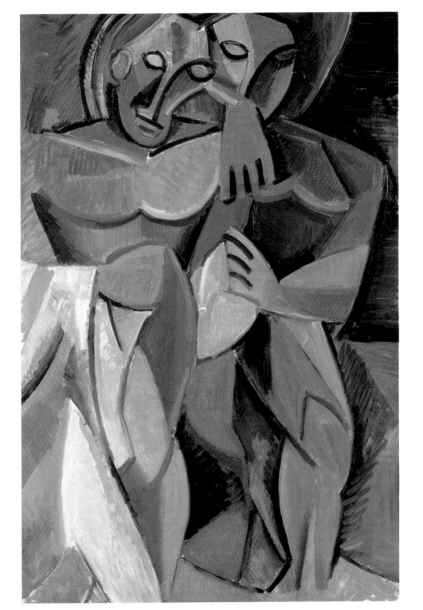

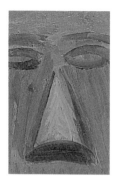

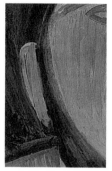

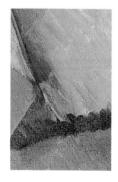

With the *Naked Youth*, Picasso wanted to pose the figure like a statue, solidly and weightily, in contrast, as it were, with its relaxed, flowing stance, its displaced centre of gravity and the light tonality dissolving the sharpness of form. But while the youth's naked body recalls a warm, pink Greek marble and the ideal of antique harmony, his solid figure with its large hands and feet is closer to the image of a peasant youth, to those descendants of an ancient Mediterranean race that Picasso would encounter in the summer of 1906 in Gosol, in the Spanish Pyrenees.

The Farmer (Half-Length)

1908
oil on canvas, 81 x 65 cm
The Hermitage, St. Petersburg

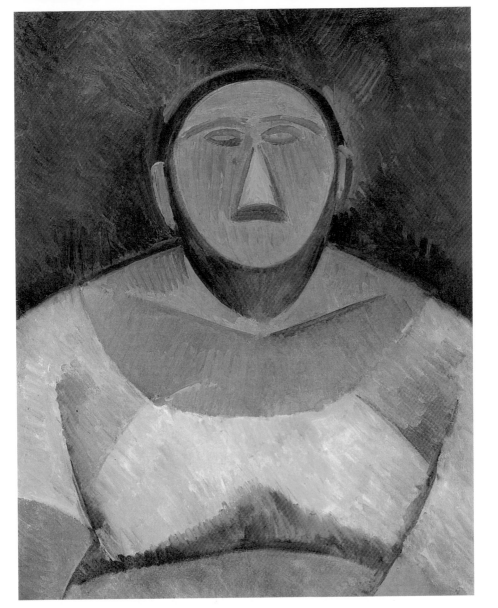

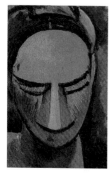

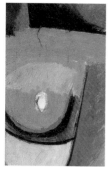

His trip to Spain was in itself very significant during that period of returning to his Mediterranean sources; the time spent in Gosol, a tiny mountain village near Andorra, is doubly important, for it shows clearly the sources and the emotions underlying the fascination with archaic Iberian art that so intrigued Picasso in the autumn of 1906 in Paris.

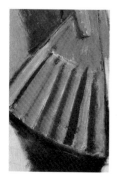

Woman with Fan (After the Ball)

1908
oil on canvas, 150 x 100 cm
The Hermitage, St. Petersburg

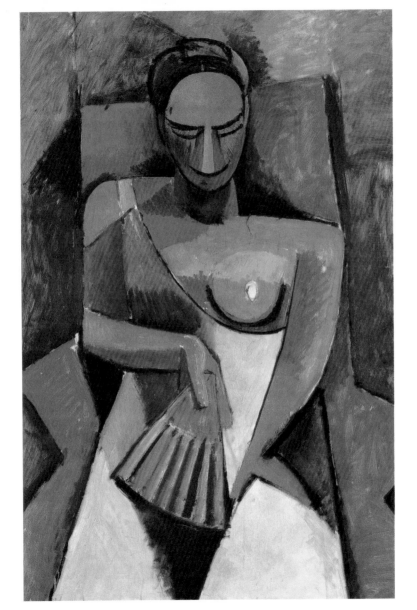

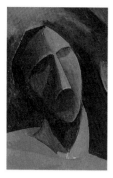

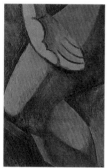

Gosol was for Picasso, probably, a second Horta de Ebro, the village where he had spent about a year when he was seventeen. Continuing and delving deeper into the theme of youthful nakedness, Picasso now found his source not so much in the ephebic type, as in the architectonics of simplified plastic forms.

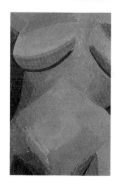

Nude in a Landscape (The Dryad)

1908
oil on canvas, 185 x 108 cm
The Hermitage, St. Petersburg

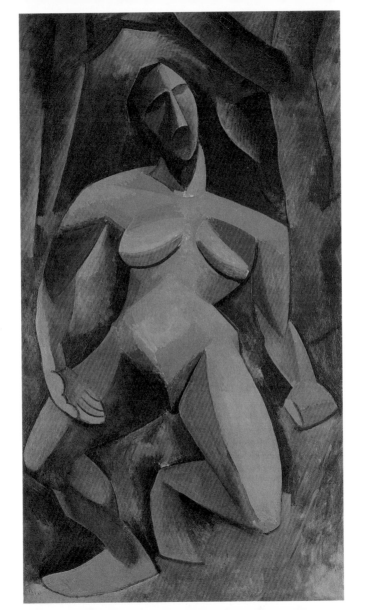

139

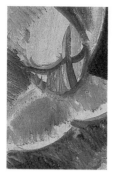

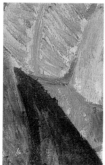

As is evident from *Still-Life with Porrón*, the Gosol works reflect a subconscious, but logical growth of two basic trends in the development of the artist's formal conception: the underlining of the original expressive simplicity of volumes and the increasingly complex compositional structure of the whole.

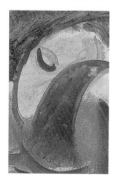

Bathers

1908
oil on canvas, 38 x 62.5 cm
The Hermitage, St. Petersburg

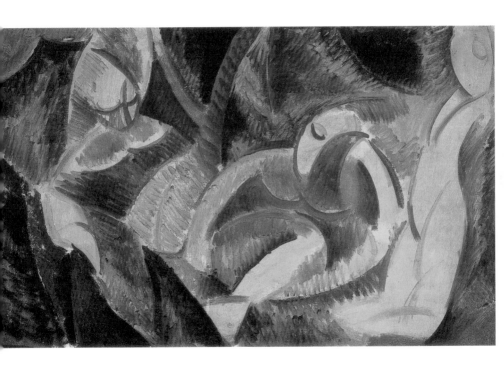

141

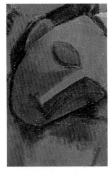

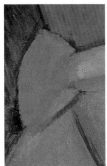

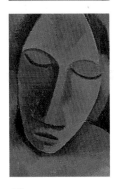

These trends acquired their greatest stylistic expression in Paris during Autumn 1906, coinciding with Picasso's discovery of then recently unearthed archaic Iberian sculpture exhibited in the Louvre, and E1 Greco paintings, which Picasso saw with new eyes as a primarily visionary kind of art.

Three Women

1908
oil on canvas, 200 x 185 cm
The Hermitage, St. Petersburg

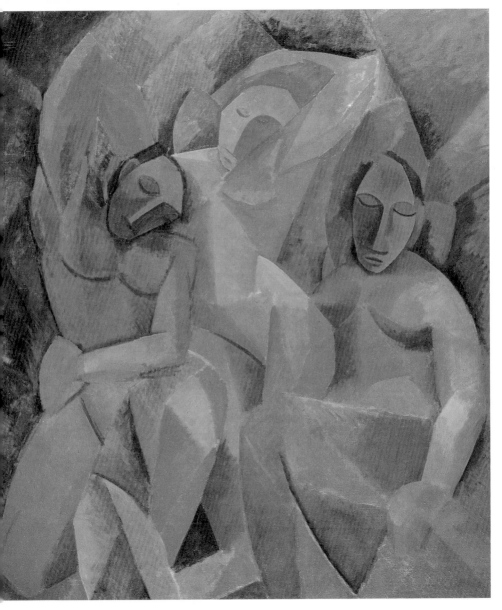

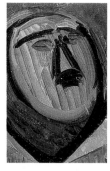

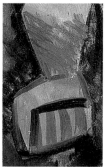

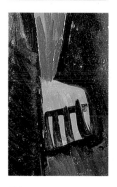

In Gosol, in the summer of 1906 the nude female form assumed an extraordinary importance for Picasso – a depersonalized, aboriginal, simple nakedness, like the concept "woman" (see *Two Nudes; Seated Nude with Her Legs Crossed; Standing Nude*).

Peasant Woman (Full-Length)

1908
oil on canvas, 81 x 56 cm
The Hermitage, St. Petersburg

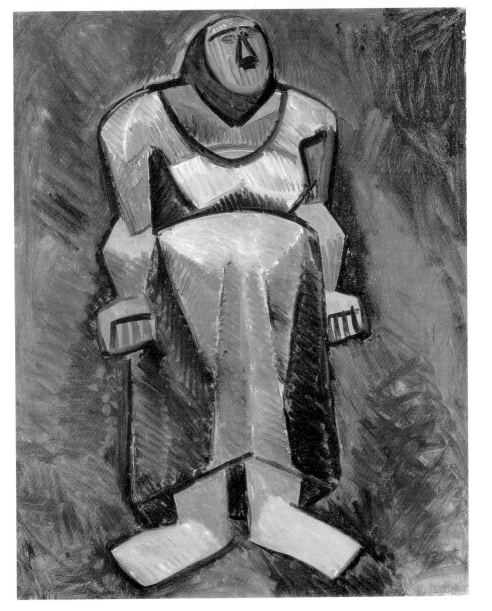

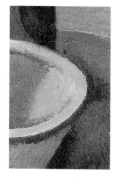

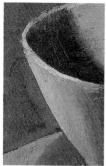

From the viewpoint of the artist's internal world, their meaning was undoubtedly far more profound than a simple artistic expression, and that is confirmed by the importance that female nudes were to assume as subjects for Picasso in the winter and spring of 1907, when he developed the composition of the large painting that came to be known as *Les Demoiselles d'Avignon.*

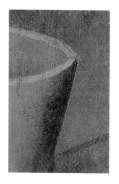

Pitcher and Bowls

1908
oil on cardboard, 66 x 50.5 cm
The Hermitage, St. Petersburg

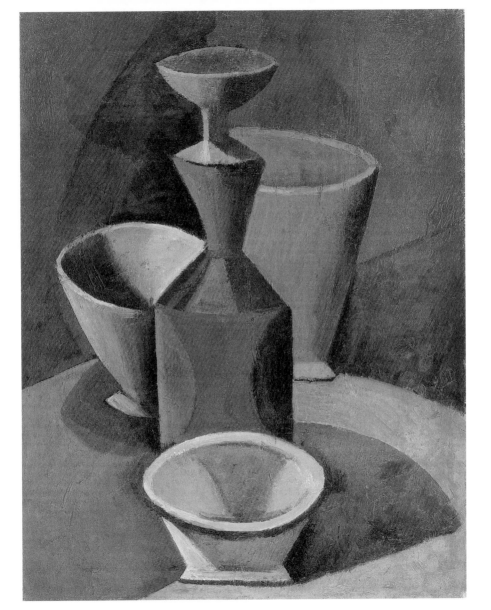

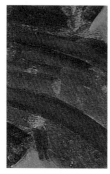

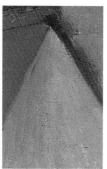

Hastily leaving Gosol because of an outbreak of typhus, Picasso returned to Paris with his head shaved bald. Perhaps that led him to depict himself in the famous *Self-portrait with a Palette* from the autumn of 1906 as a juvenile, youthful Adam-the-artist.

On 25 October 1906, Picasso turned twenty-five. That date marks the completion of one full cycle in his artistic development. Working in the spring of 1907 on *Les Demoiselles d'Avignon*, he was born anew as a painter.

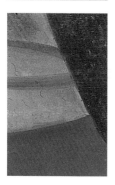

House and Trees (House in a Garden)

1908
oil on canvas, 73 x 61 cm
The Hermitage, St. Petersburg

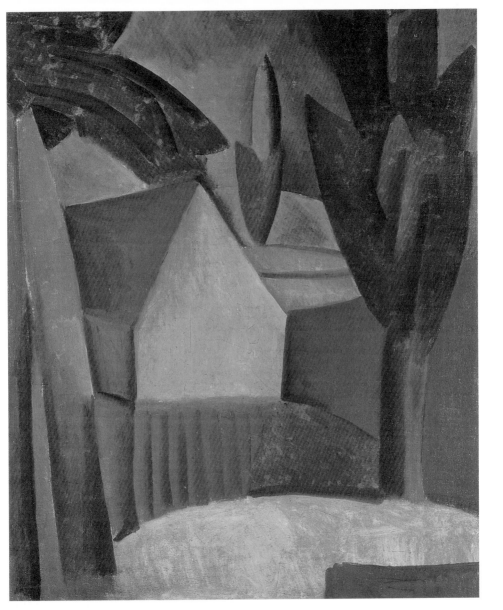

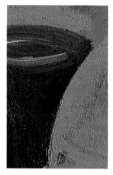

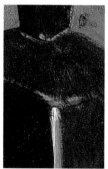

The young artists of the early twentieth century undoubtedly demonstrated an avant-garde spirit of aesthetic radicalism. Yet even the leader of the Fauves, Matisse, was scandalized when he visited Picasso and saw *Les Demoiselles d'Avignon*; to him the painting was an abuse of modern art, as he could find no aesthetically justified explanation for it. Many of its first viewers, at any rate, saw it as something Assyrian.

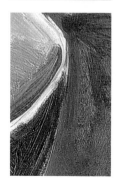

Green Bowl and Black Bottle

1908
oil on canvas, 61 x 50.5 cm
The Hermitage, St. Petersburg

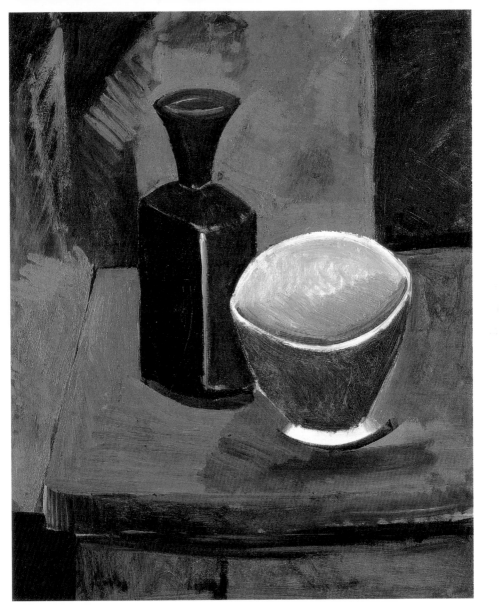

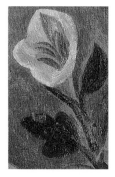

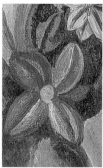

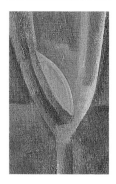

This was a solitary, internal revolution, and perhaps nobody ever understood it as well as Apollinaire, who went through the same kind of rupture and revolution one year later. What did Picasso gain at the price of forgetting, with such difficulty, his former vision based on classic pictorial tradition? A new understanding of the plastic arts, in which their formal language stands in the same relationship to the forms of the visible world as poetic language stands to everyday speech.

Bunch of Flowers in a Grey Jug

1908
oil on canvas, 81 x 65 cm
The Hermitage, St. Petersburg

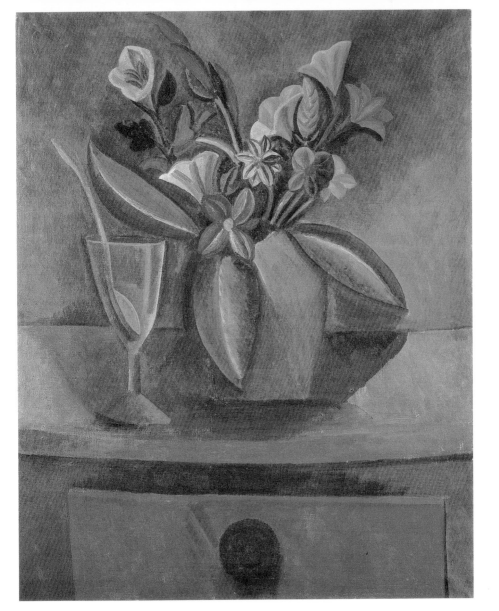

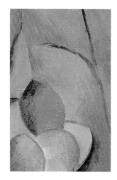

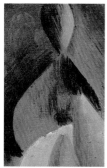

Locked up in his studio, working through the night as was his habit, Picasso stubbornly concentrated on learning anew, changing his taste, re-educating his personal feelings. "In those times I worked completely without any models. What I was looking for was something very different," Picasso wrote to Daix. He was seeking the power of expression, not in the subject matter, the theme or the object *per se*, but in the lines, colours, forms, strokes and brushwork taken in their own independent meaning, in the energy of the pictorial handwriting.

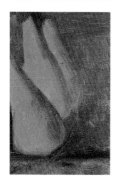

Bowl with Fruit and Wineglass
(Still-Life with Bowl and Fruit)

1908-1909
oil on canvas, 92 x 72.5 cm
The Hermitage, St. Petersburg

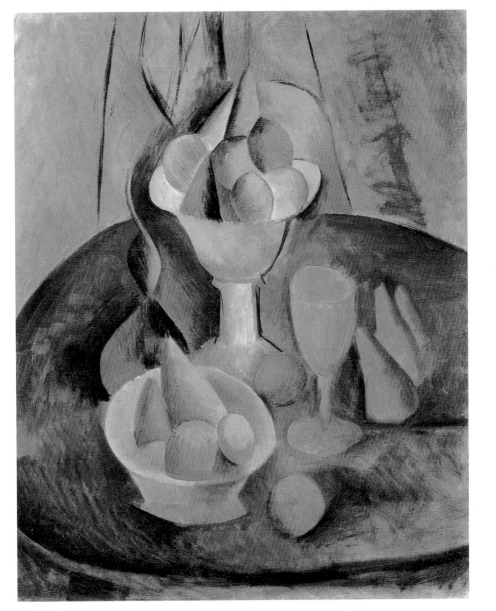

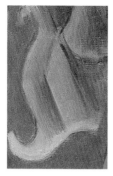

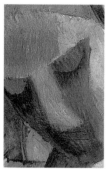

On the one hand, the awkwardness and monstrosity of certain 1907 pictures served to re-educate feeling, while, on the other, they corresponded to Picasso's pictorial philosophy at the time. They both activated his emotional perceptions and imbued the image (thanks to their archaic associations) with a certain timeless atmosphere, a certain eternal background. André Malraux recalls Picasso's words concerning the need "to always work against, even against oneself", and that, it seems, was also a discovery of the period.

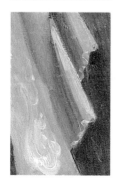

Queen Isabeau

1908-1909
oil on canvas, 92 x 73 cm
The Pushkin Museum of Fine Arts, Moscow

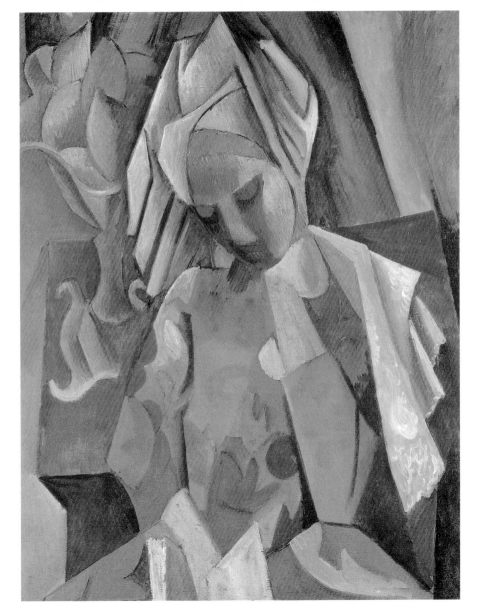

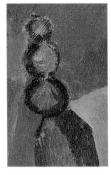

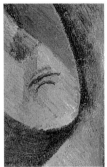

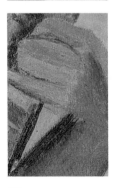

Among the great pictorial revelations of 1907 we find two masterpieces in the Hermitage collection: *The Dance of the Veils (Nude with Drapery)* and *Composition with a Skull. The Dance of the Veils* has traditionally – but groundlessly – been regarded in the context of African influences; the entire year of 1907 is referred to as the African period.

Woman with a Mandolin

———————————————

1908-1909
oil on canvas, 91 x 72.5 cm
The Hermitage, St. Petersburg

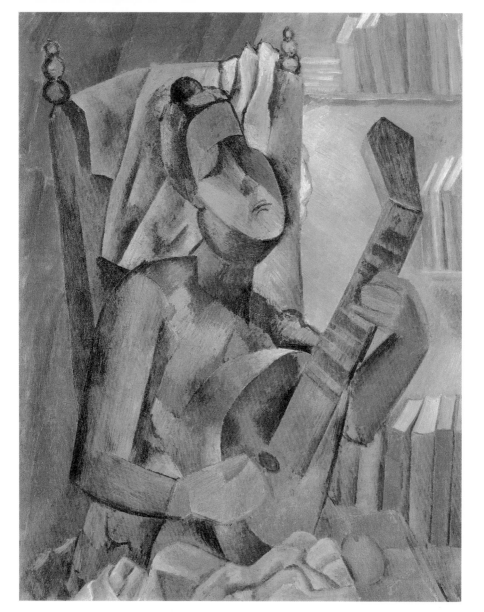

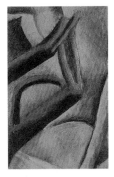

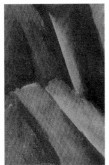

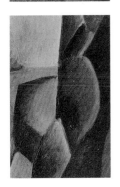

However, Picasso's "barbarism" of 1907 is not ethnographic in character, it is negativistic; a "working against, even against oneself", as he was to say later. *The Dance of the Veils* is polemically oriented on the European tradition of painting; it is literally full of various associations with that tradition, more often than not contradicting it.

House in a Garden (House and Trees)

1909
oil on canvas, 92 x 73 cm
The Pushkin Museum of Fine Arts, Moscow

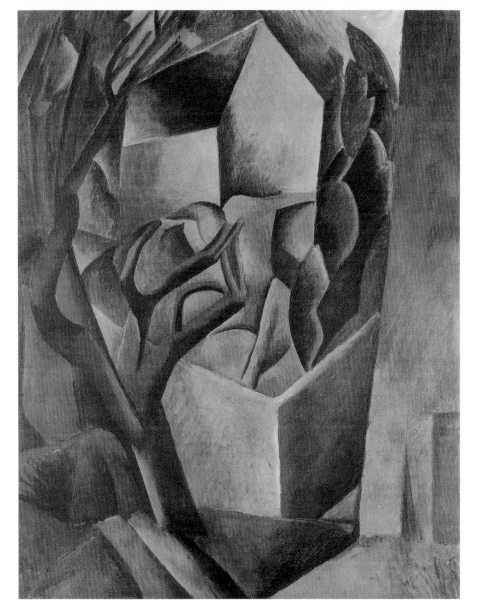

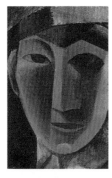

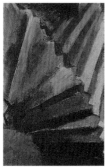

The same link with the European pictorial tradition, if not as simply discernible, is imbedded in the concept of the *Composition with a Skull*, which is often, and not without reason, interpreted as Picasso's original variation on the Vanitas theme, so widespread in traditional Western painting.

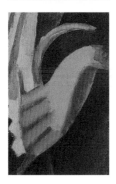

Lady with a Fan

1909
oil on canvas, 101 x 81 cm
The Pushkin Museum of Fine Arts, Moscow

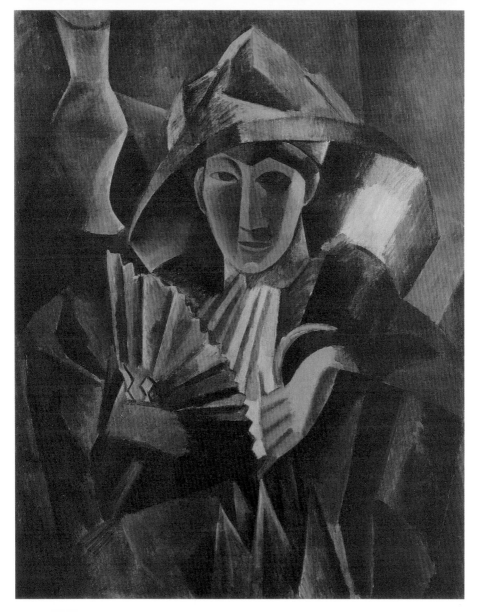

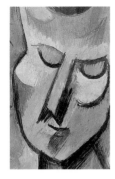

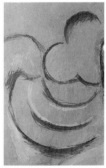

It is not sufficient to understand the revolutionary upheaval of 1907 only as a search for untraditional formal approaches to traditional themes in art, only as a renewal of the language of the visual arts. The main achievement of Picasso's creative spirit was the poetic metaphor, that is to say the creation of an image based on the most unexpected associations, on the interplay and power of imagination.

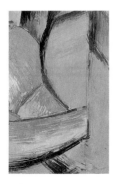

Man with Crossed Arms

1909
watercolour, gouache and charcoal on
paper pasted on cardboard, 65.2 x 49.2 cm
The Hermitage, St. Petersburg

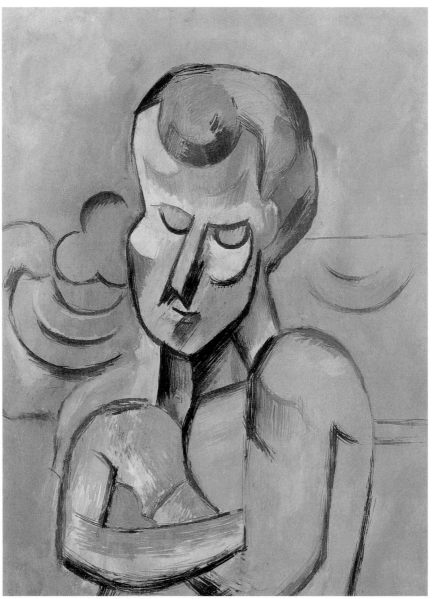

165

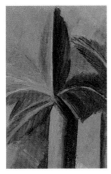

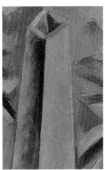

The development of this new poetry would, during the Cubist period, lead to such startling inventions as the inclusion of words as images in a visual context.

In spite of the attention paid over the past decade to Picasso's so-called early Cubist work and all the efforts made to achieve some order in the understanding of his evolution, the clarity one would like to see in the general comprehension of the period of 1907-1908 is still lacking.

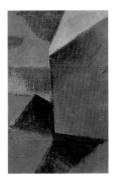

Factory in Horta de Ebro

1909
oil on canvas, 53 x 60 cm
The Hermitage, St. Petersburg

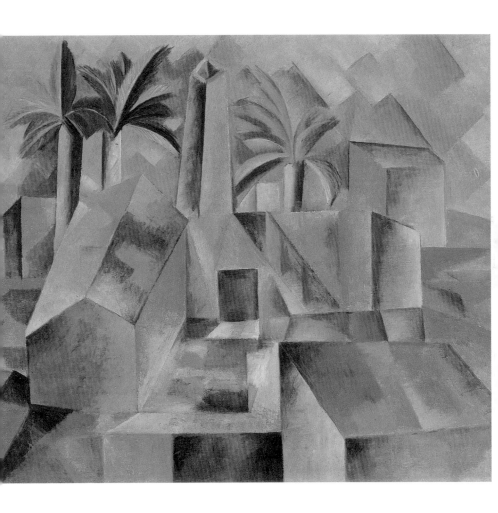

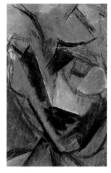

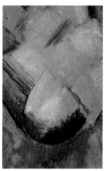

The formal approach, the preconceived view of works of that period as being proto-Cubist or pre-Cubist does not allow scholars to assess the artist in his full significance. Yet it was precisely in 1908, at the height of "proto-Cubism", that visitors to Picasso's studio heard him speak not "of values and volumes", but "of the subjective and of the emotions and instinct."

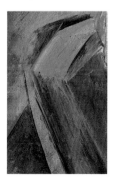

Nude Woman Sitting
in an Armchair (Young Woman)

1909
oil on canvas, 100 x 73 cm
Centre Georges Pompidou, Paris

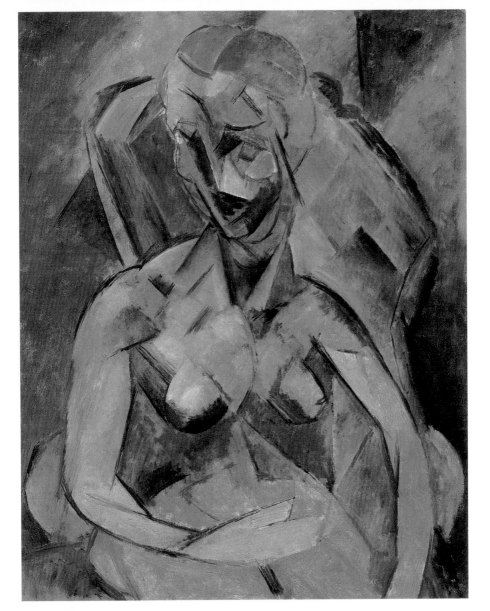

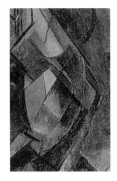

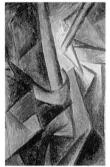

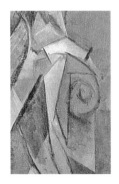

If one leaves aside the concept of proto-Cubism and looks upon the creative material of 1908 as a single entity, ignoring differences in sizes and techniques between paintings, sculpture, and minor sketches, then one sees their organic unity as a monumental ensemble. Turning from the paintings to the original ideas – sketches, drafts, studies – one sees everywhere not simply figurative compositions but, as it were, depictions of certain events, ideas for subjects, each with its own internal dramaturgy.

Woman Seated in an Armchair

1909-1910
oil on canvas, 100 x 73 cm
Centre Georges Pompidou, Paris

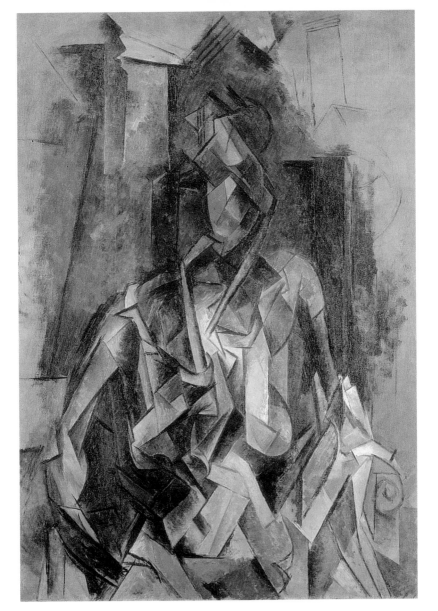

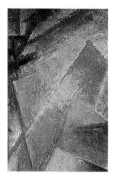

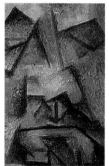

It seems as though the new form itself – built on the expressive rhythm of strong, sinuous lines, on sharp, clean, articulated planes, on the internal equilibrium of the entire pictorial structure – this morphologically clear and monumentally impressive form – produced in the artist's imagination impersonal, timeless, powerful images.

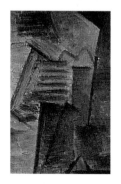

Portrait of Ambroise Vollard

1910
oil on canvas, 93 x 66 cm
The Pushkin Museum of Fine Arts, Moscow

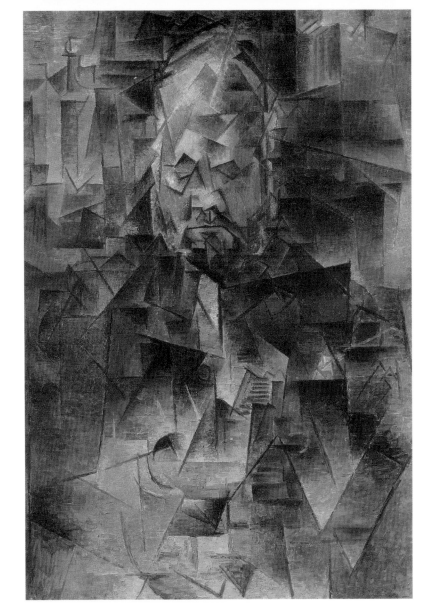

173

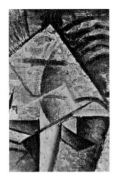

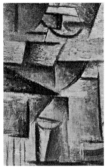

What could be vaguely felt in the works of 1907 as something existing before time, as some background to eternity, now, thanks to the characteristics of form, becomes objective reality. Deeply involved throughout 1907 in the development of a new plastic anatomy for his painting, an anatomy based on the material of the human figure, Picasso imperceptibly, instinctively uncovers and then grasps the corporal-psychological differences of structure between the male and the female archetype.

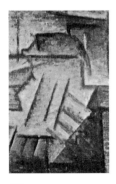

Portrait of Henri Kahnweiler

1910
oil on canvas, 101 x 63.5 cm
Art Institute of Chicago, Chicago

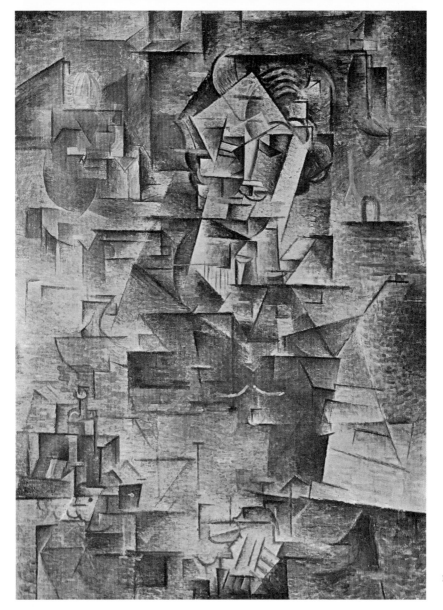

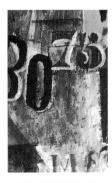

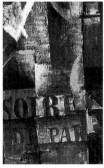

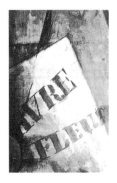

Basic morphological structure helps him to grasp the metaphorically expressed essential truth of natural phenomena.

The reason for, and meaning of Picasso's proto-Cubism is normally explained as the artist's desire to radically simplify his pictorial vision of the objective world, to strip away the layers of illusion and reveal its constructive physical essence.

Violin, Wineglass, Pipe and Inkpot

1912
oil on canvas, 81 x 54 cm
Narodni Galerie, Prague

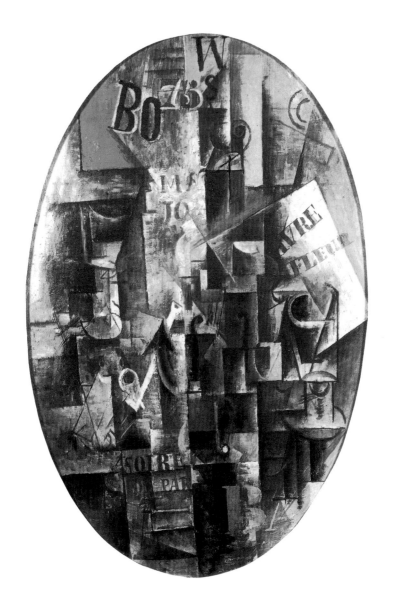

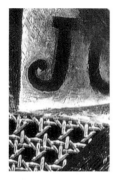

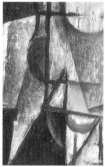

It is usual in this context to cite the famous words Cézanne wrote in a letter addressed to the artist Emile Bernard that was published in the autumn of 1907: "Treat nature by means of cylinder, sphere, cone." Another of the generally assumed points of departure for so-called proto-Cubism is the African influence, which introduced simplification of anatomy and other expressive features.

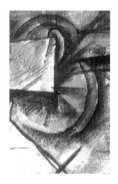

Still life with Chair Caning

1912
collage of oil, oilcloth, and pasted paper
simulating chair caning on canvas, 29 x 37 cm
Musée Picasso, Paris

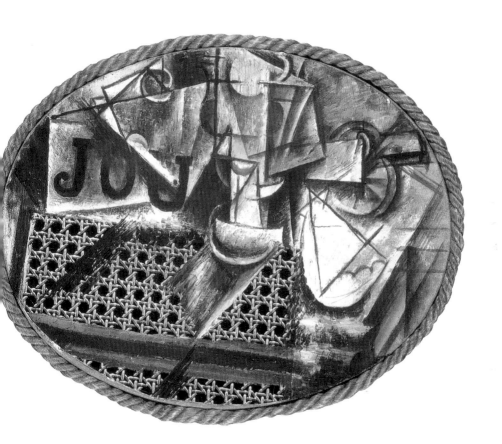

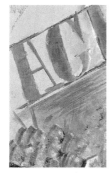

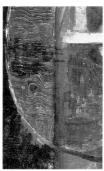

The combination of these two diametrically opposed influences – Cézanne's "perceptualized" art and Africa's "conceptualised" art – is usually employed to explain the stylistic phenomenon of proto-Cubism as an art entirely preoccupied with the problem of space.

Yet when we dig deeper into the sources of Picasso's creative ideas – the sketchbooks of early 1908 – we find not objective reality geometrized for geometrization's sake, but rather a desire to lend adequate expression to the artist's subjective truth.

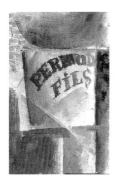

Bottle of Pernod and Wineglass
(Table in a Café)

_____

1912
oil on canvas, 45.5 x 32.5 cm
The Hermitage, St. Petersburg

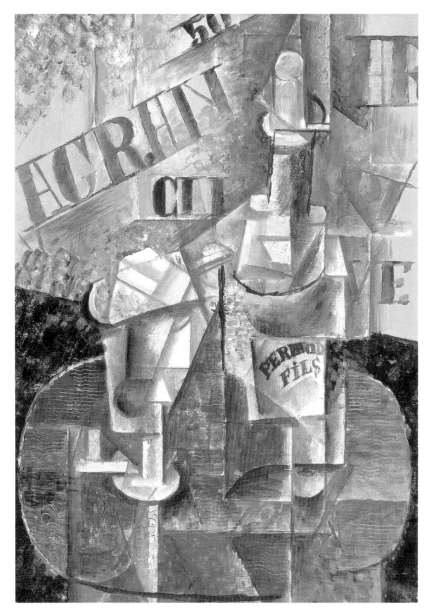

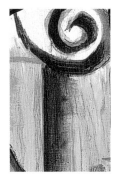

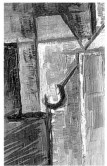

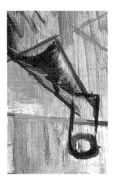

Picasso's proto-Cubism – coming as it did not from the external appearance of events and things, but from great emotional and instinctive feelings, from the most profound layers of the psyche – clairvoyantly arrived at the suprapersonal and thereby borders on the archaic mythological consciousness.

The key work in which both the formal and the pictorial issues of Picasso's proto-Cubism were concentrated was his major canvas of 1908, *Three Women*.

Violin

———

1912
oil on canvas, 55 x 46 cm
The Pushkin Museum of Fine Arts, Moscow

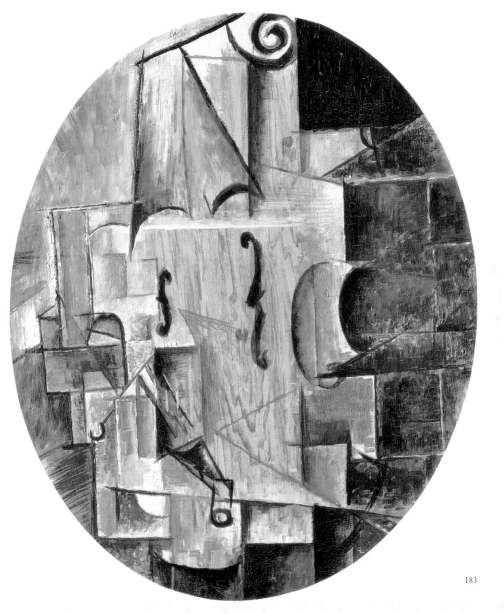

183

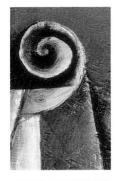

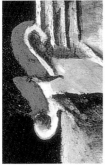

In that painting, all that remains of the original concept of forest bathers is the general structure of the three-figure group on the right and the colour scheme. Studying these figures, one must not ignore the differences which subtly but unequivocally separate one from the other in spite of their apparent homogeneity. The compositional and conceptual unity and the internal dramaturgy of this strange scene, steeped in torpor, are built on their correlations.

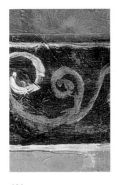

Violin and Guitar

1913
oil on canvas, 65 x 54 cm
The Hermitage, St. Petersburg

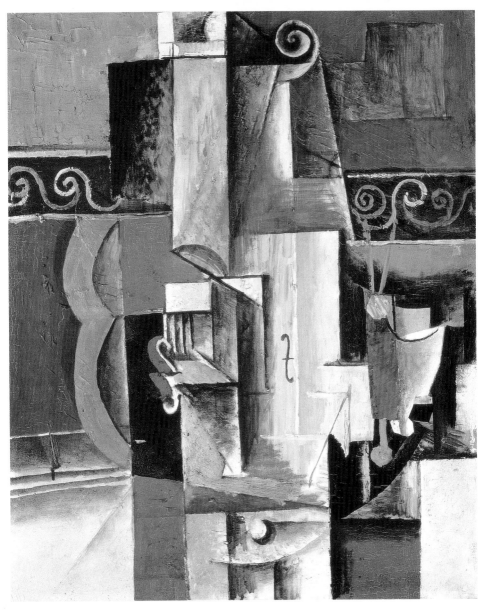

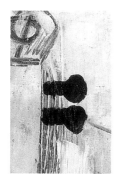

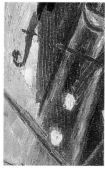

Thus, Picasso's interest in reproducing volumes on a flat surface was inseparable in 1908 from sculpture, and it was not before 1909 that the artist came into contact with Cézanne's purely pictorial experience, moving from the colouring of flat planes, inclined this way and that, to the modulation of volume by means of minute, form-creating daubs.

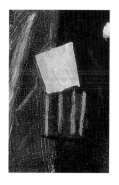

Clarinet and Violin

1913
oil on canvas, 55 x 33 cm
The Hermitage, St. Petersburg

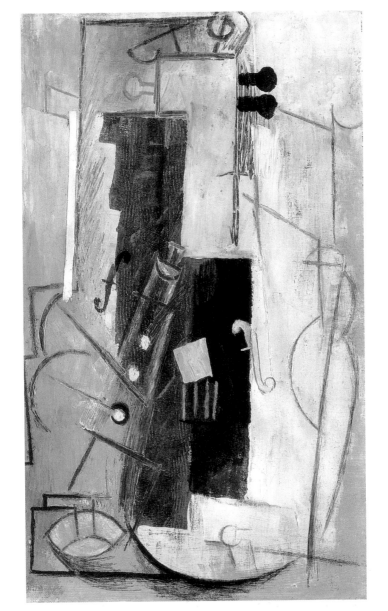

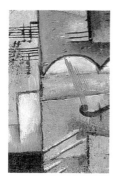

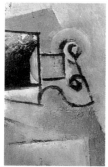

The form of *Three Women* seems to be a sculptor's creation. As for *Peasant Woman* (full-length), with its powerfully hewn volumes and mass that seems to be charged with dynamite, it originated directly from work on a carved statue. For Picasso sculpture also served to verify the feeling of reality, in the sense of physical validity, since for him "sculpture is the best comment that a painter can make on painting."

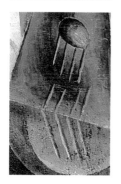

Musical Instruments

1913
ripolin, oil, plaster, sawdust on oilcloth, 98 x 80 cm (oval)
The Hermitage, St. Petersburg

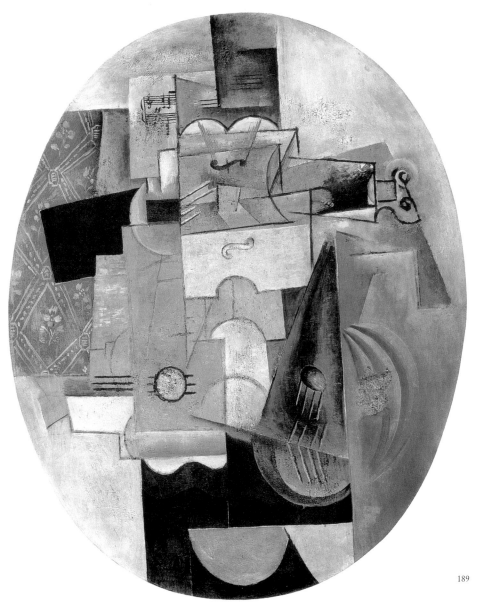

189

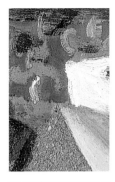

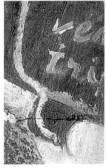

In the summer of 1908, Picasso at first turned to the still-life genre because of his depressed state of mind and a desire to find support in the world of simple realities. Later his inquisitive and creative penetration into the specifics of how painting might represent objective realities opened the way to a completely new method of plastic representation, called Cubism.

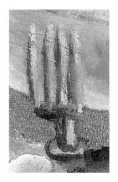

Tavern (The Ham)
_____

1914
oil and sawdust on cardboard, 29.5 x 38 cm (oval)
The Hermitage, St. Petersburg

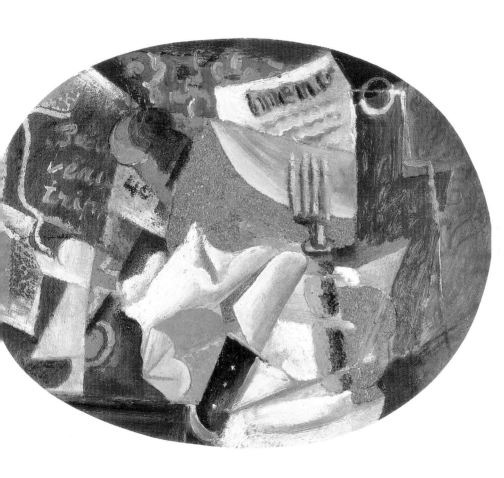

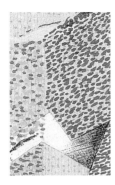

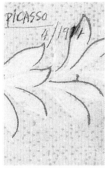

It is not accidental that the still-life genre, with its concrete space, became the favourite subject of Cubist painting. No other genre was so conducive to a concentrated analytical inquiry into the structural principles of the stable forms in a spatial ensemble.

The absence of exact dates, which makes it impossible to determine the absolute chronology of Picasso's proto-Cubism, is perhaps most vexatious for the period between his stay in La Rue-des-Bois in August 1908 and his departure for Horta de Ebro at the end of the spring of 1909.

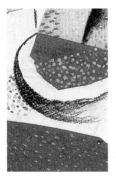

Composition Bowl of Fruit and Sliced Pear

1914
wallpaper, gouache and plumbago on cardboard, 35 x 32 cm
The Hermitage, St. Petersburg

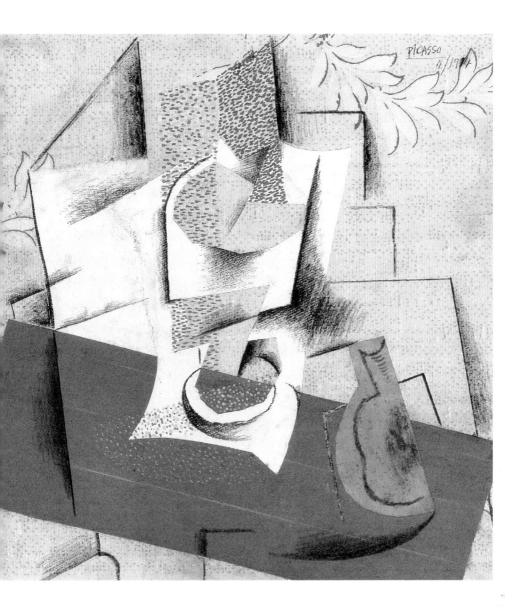

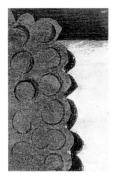

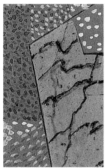

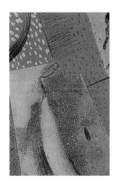

When one considers as a whole all that was done over these eight months – that is, everything created on the very threshold of Cubism – one sees the artist's thoughts flowing in many directions, some of which led to and synthesized new trends, while others temporarily disappeared below the surface.

Bowl of Fruit with Bunch of Grapes
and Sliced Pear

1914
paper, gouache, pencil and sawdust on cardboard
67.6 x 57.2 cm
The Hermitage, St. Petersburg

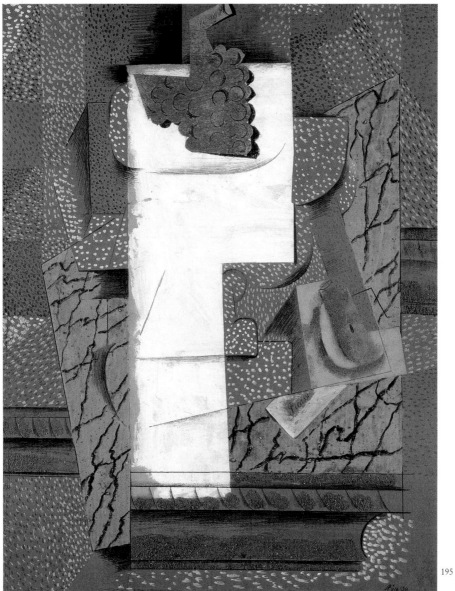

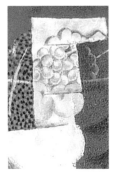

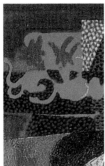

Having a *post factum* knowledge of what might be called the ideal goal of this progression, Cubism, scholars observe the accumulation in Picasso's work between the autumn of 1908 and the spring of 1909 of those formal features which mark the "most important and certainly the most complete and radical artistic revolution since the Renaissance"

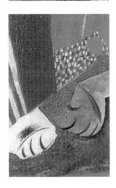

Portrait of a Young Girl
(Woman Seated in Front of a Fireplace)

1914
oil on canvas, 130 x 96.5 cm
Centre Georges Pompidou, Paris

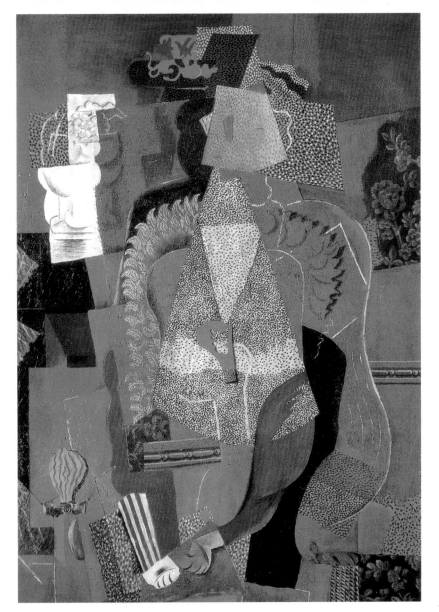

197

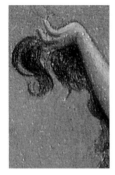

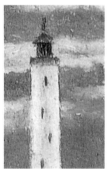

Just as African art is usually considered the factor leading to the development of Picasso's classic aesthetics in 1907, the lessons of Cézanne are perceived as the cornerstone of this new progression.

Georges Braque, with whom Picasso became friends in the autumn of 1908 and together with whom he led Cubism during the six years of its apogee, was amazed by the similarity of Picasso's pictorial experiments to his own; he explained that Cubism's main direction was the materialization of space.

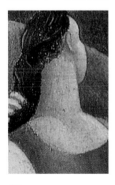

The Bathers

1918
oil on canvas, 26.3 x 21.7 cm
Musée Picasso, Paris

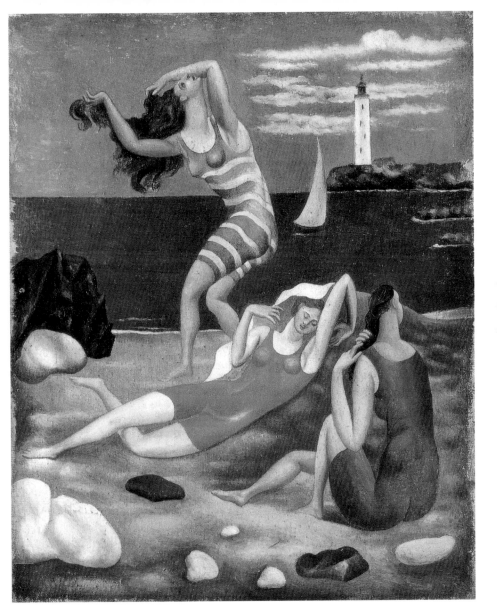

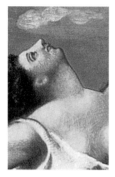

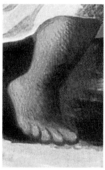

His penchant for the pictorial, his discovery of Douanier Rousseau as an example of the primitive consciousness, unspoiled by academic aesthetics, and also the beginning of his friendship with Braque ("It was as if we were married," Picasso said) which ended his creative solitude... All these factors made Picasso more receptive than before to the purely pictorial solution of painters, past and present.

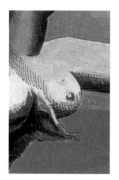

Women Running on the Beach

1922
gouache on plywood, 32.5 x 42.1 cm
Musée Picasso, Paris

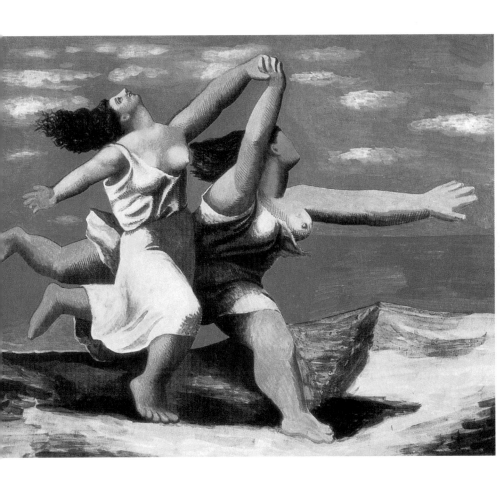

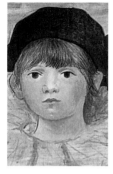

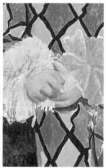

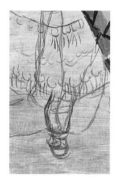

Thus, the Hermitage *Nude in a Landscape*, coming from a series crucially important to Analytical Cubism, seems to be an answer to Matisse's tendency to transform the figure into a flat, coloured arabesque – an organic part of the ripening decorative grand style. Conversely, Picasso is interested in the figure *per se*, the figure as a bodily apparatus which in itself is a powerful tool of expression, as Tugendhold put it so well.

Paul as Harlequin

1924
oil on canvas, 190 x 97.5 cm
Musée Picasso, Paris

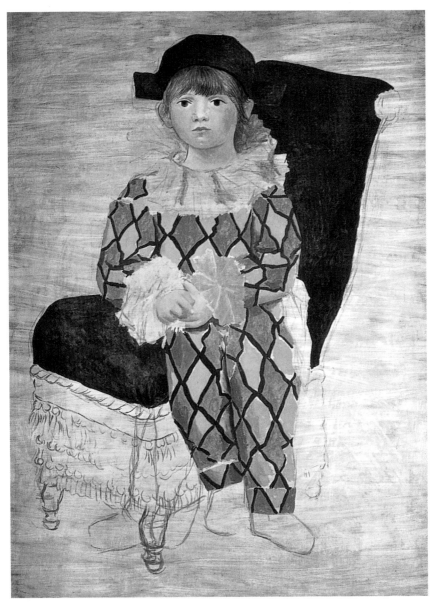

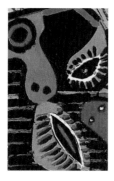

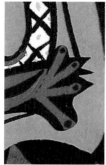

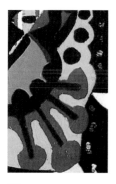

"The goal I proposed myself in making Cubism? To paint and nothing more. And to paint seeking a new expression, divested of useless realism, with a method linked only to my thought – without enslaving myself with objective reality." If the artist spoke of a quest for new expression, it is because that was his professional concern – to find adequate means of expression, an adequate language for the impulses inherent in his thinking.

The Kiss

1925
oil on canvas, 130.5 x 97.7 cm
Musée Picasso, Paris

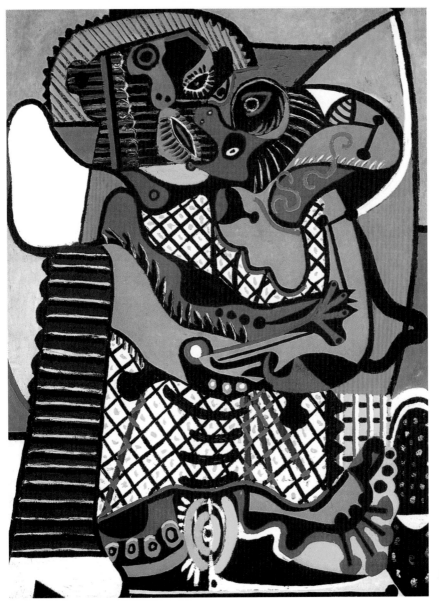

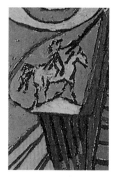

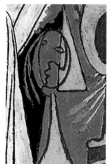

Referring to the transformation of the composition *Carnival at the Bistro* into the still-life *Bread and Bowl of Fruit on a Table,* Pierre Daix believes Picasso "could not have better expressed the thought that, at that stage, every object or character is, above all, a certain spatial rhythm, a three-dimensional structure which plays its role in the composition through what it brings to the pictorial structure of the whole and not through its own reality."

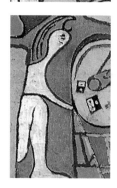

The Crucifixion

—————————

1930
oil on plywood, 51.5 x 66.5 cm
Musée Picasso, Paris

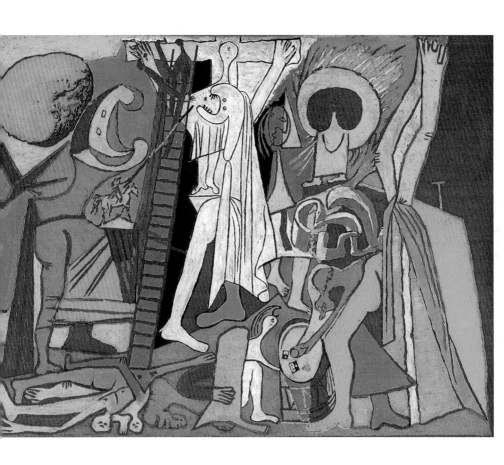

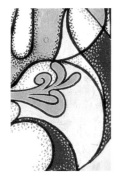

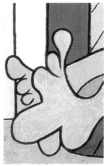

Such views, however, are hardly correct, for Picasso at that stage was still very far from abstraction. Nevertheless, the characteristics of Picasso's objects and figures invariably relate to an internal meaning, as is apparent, for instance, in *Queen Isabeau*, *Lady with a Fan* and also *Woman with a Mandolin*.

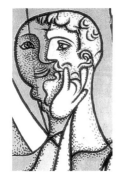

The Sculptor

———————

1931
oil on plywood, 128.5 x 96 cm
Musée Picasso, Paris

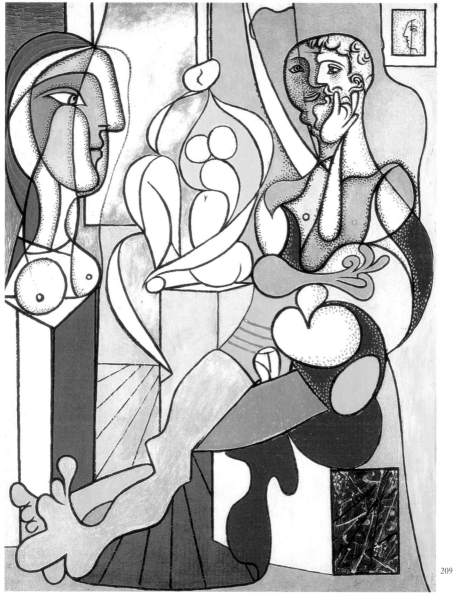

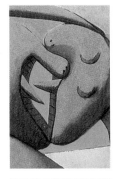

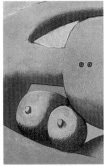

In *Woman with a Mandolin* Picasso was on the way to a discovery that would in the future radically transform the very principles of his art – the image presented as a visual metaphor. He stood on the threshold of the discovery of plastic poetry. The evolution of Picasso's Cubism was to assume a certain measure of consistency and logic beginning with the canvases completed after the summer spent at Horta de Ebro in 1909.

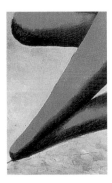

Figures on the Beach

———————————

1931
oil on canvas, 130 x 195 cm
Musée Picasso, Paris

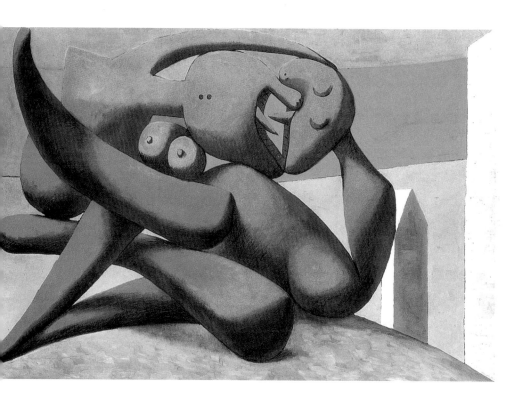

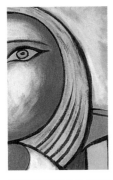

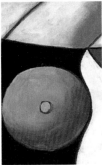

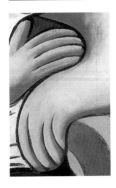

Such paintings as *Factory* are considered classics of Analytical Cubism.

In Horta Picasso felt reality with his entire body, with all his senses, with his very conscience; his art once more made contact with his environment. This contact was, however, affected with the help of his new "optics": they were amazingly purist in their simplicity and clarity.

The Lecture
—————
1932
oil on canvas, 130 x 97.5 cm
Musée Picasso, Paris

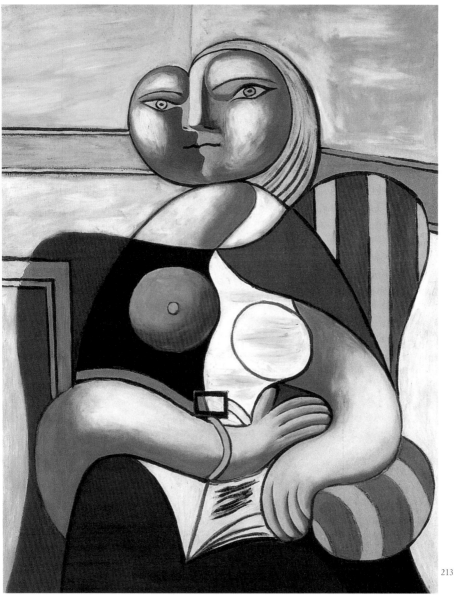

213

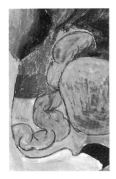

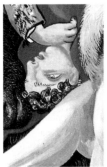

They excluded the accidental, the formless and the secondary; they brought order to nature's chaos and at the same time sharpened to the limit the version of form as the interplay of spatial contrasts, turning a scene into a rich panorama of different aspects arranged according to the character of the subject. They were to serve as the basis of Cubism's formal vocabulary.

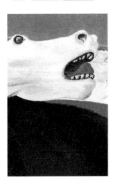

The Bullfight

1933
oil on canvas, 31.2 x 40.3 cm
Musée Picasso, Paris

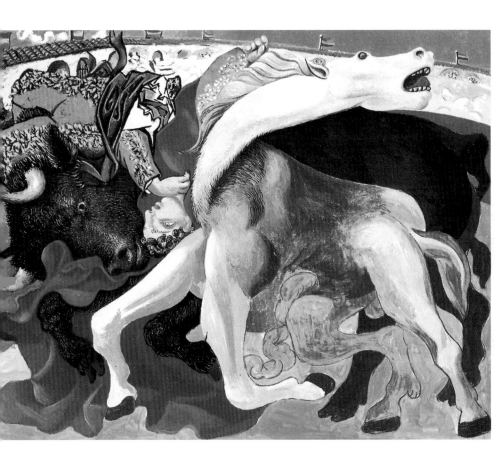

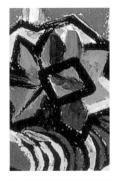

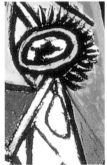

Generally considered a masterpiece of Analytical Cubism, the Moscow *Portrait of Ambroise Vollard* is a real masterpiece of psychological realism, illuminating a quality that was perceived in 1910 as one of the Spanish painter's paradoxes, when Metzinger noted: "Picasso openly declares himself a realist."

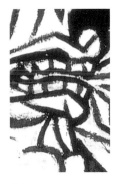

Weeping Woman
_____

1937
oil on canvas, 60 x 49 cm
Tate Gallery, London

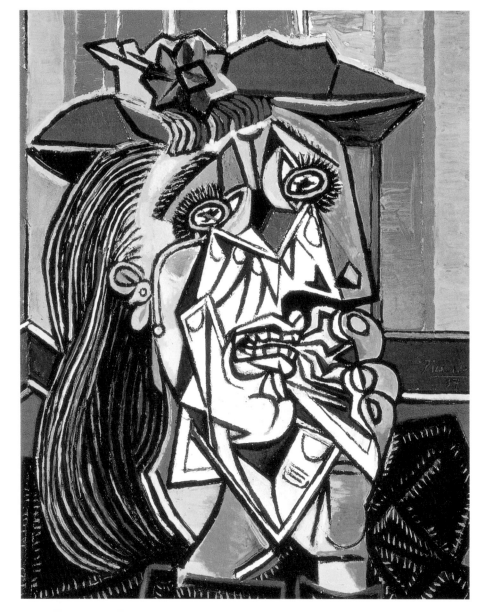

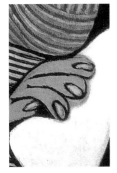

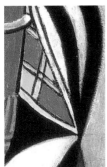

Throughout 1910 and 1911 Picasso and Braque, shoulder to shoulder, developed this hermetic art in which every picture was an autonomous slice of "pure reality" that did not imitate the environment. And even though these works had their own subjects, usually still-lifes and the figures of musicians, the reality of this kind of painting was based on more complex, and not always concrete, feelings.

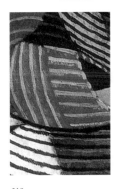

Portrait of Marie-Thérèse Walter

1937
oil on canvas, 100 x 81 cm
Musée Picasso, Paris

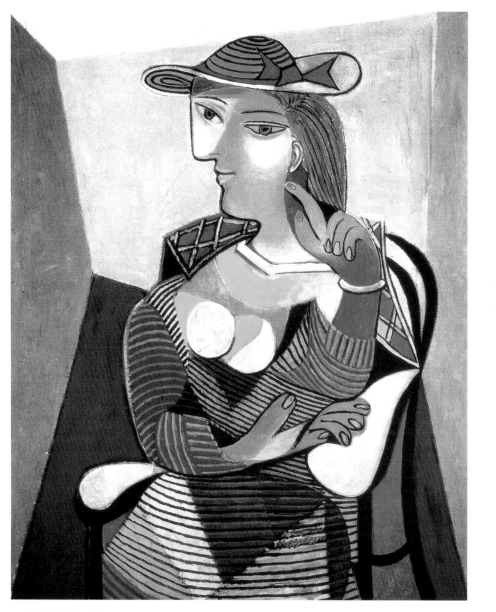

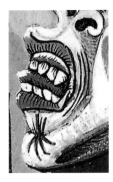

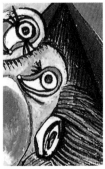

In these hermetic paintings Picasso communicated a "scent" of reality that one can grasp through visual allusions: the contours of a glass, a pipe, the elbow-rest of an armchair, the fringe of a tablecloth, a fan, the neck of a violin. Soon, in the summer of 1911, another kind of allusion from the real world entered Picasso's painting – street signs, newspaper headlines, words from book jackets, wine bottles, and tobacco labels, musical notes – all of which are thematically linked to the subject of the canvas.

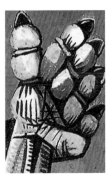

The Supplicant

1937
gouache and Chinese ink on wood
Musée Picasso, Paris

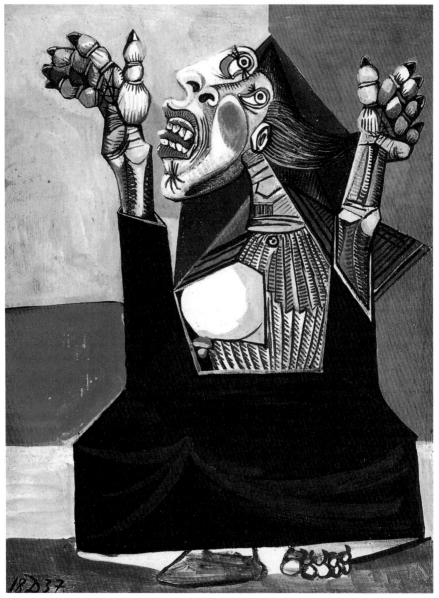

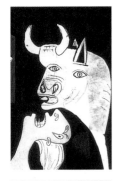

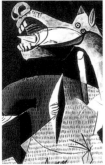

For Braque and Picasso, letters are flat forms that help create the spatial relations of the picture. They are also elements of the surrounding environment that participate in presenting the theme, supporting its subject, which they enter untransformed. Besides that, words and entire sentences, parts of words and syllables, are, to artists who live in close contact with poets, verbal images assuming meaningful relations with the painting's pictorial realities, giving the image a multiplicity of meanings.

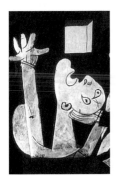

Guernica

1937
oil on canvas, 349.3 x 776.6 cm
Museo Nacional Centro de Arte Reina Sofia, Madrid

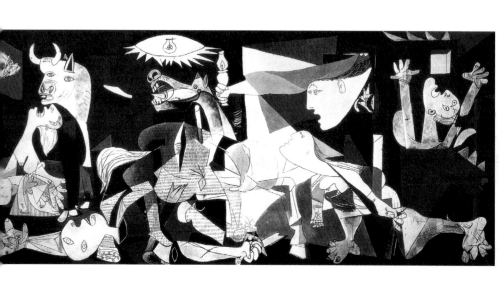

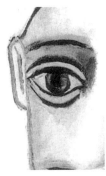

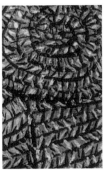

This combination of two pictorial levels also leads to the transformation of the picture into a charade with many meanings, a play on words, a total metaphor – an effect that Picasso highly prized. In the painting *Table in a Café*, created in the spring of 1912, the letters crossing the background behind the still-life are part of advertisements painted on the invisible glass panel of the café window.

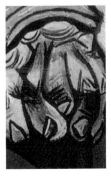

Portrait of Dora Maar

1939
oil on canvas, 81 x 65 cm
Heinz Berggruen collection, Geneva

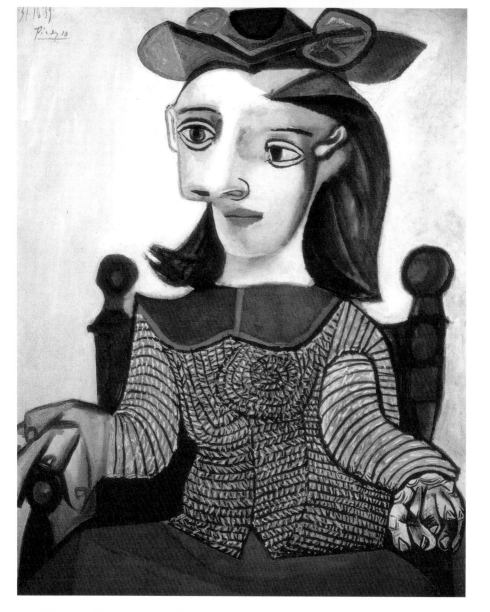

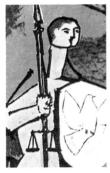

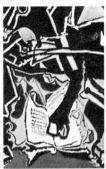

They endow the picture with the unmistakable look of modern urban life, while the motif – the bottle of Pernod and the glass with its spoon and cube of sugar, placed on the oval table – reveals Picasso's new taste for a material, concrete environment. During the first half of 1912, Picasso's Cubism underwent a mutation from Analytic to Synthetic.

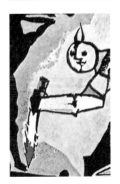

The War

1952
oil on canvas, 4.5 x 10.5 cm
Temple de la Paix, Vallauris

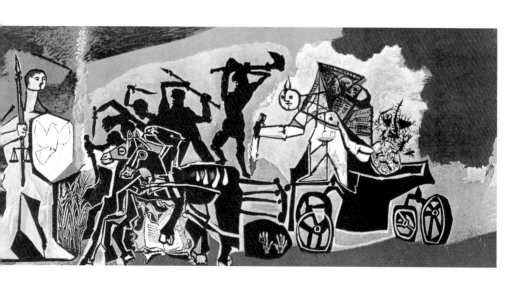

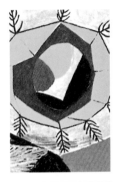

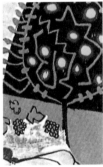

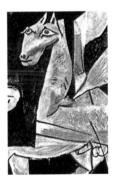

Somewhere at the very start of the year Picasso felt the need to work with tangible forms of reality – to sculpt. At the same time, his introduction into painting of letters and slogans as naked facts of reality opened the way to other facts of reality: in particular, the gluing on of different materials with their own ready-made printed forms, textures, ornaments – and so the collage technique appears.

The Peace

1952
oil on canvas, 4.5 x 10.5 cm
Temple de la Paix, Vallauris

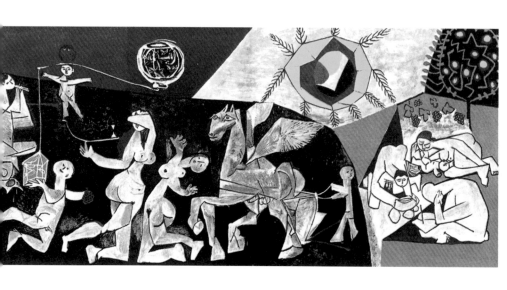

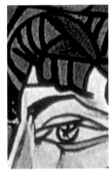

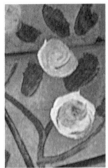

The appearance of reality – so direct and unequivocal – signalled the end of the illusory, hermetic and anonymous style of painting called Analytical Cubism, which Picasso developed for a year and a half in such intimate contact with Braque.

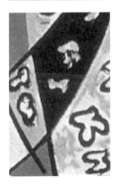

Portrait of Jacqueline with Flowers

1954
oil on canvas, 146 x 114 cm
Heirs of Jaqueline Picasso

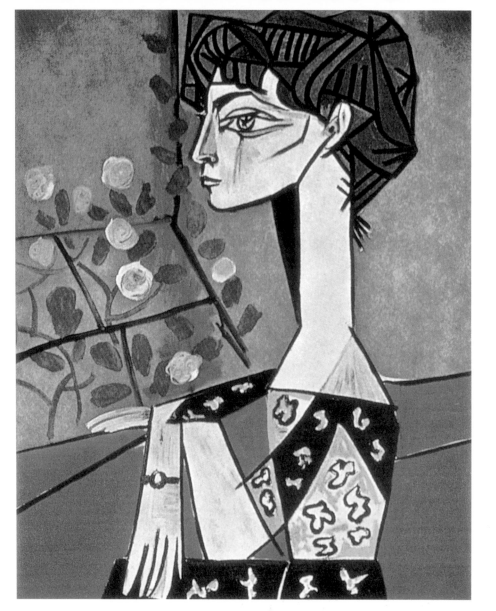

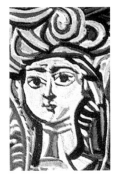

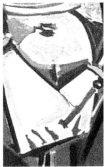

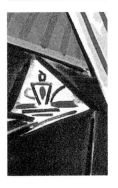

The essence of Picasso's creative genius differs from that usually associated with the notion of *"artiste-peintre"*, although, as Picasso himself put it, he "led the life of a painter" from very early childhood, and although he expressed himself through the plastic arts for eighty uninterrupted years, it might be more correct to consider him an artist-poet because his lyricism, his psyche, his gift for the metaphoric transformation of reality are no less inherent in his visual art than they are in the mental imagery of a poet.

Women of Algiers (after Delacroix)

1955
oil on canvas, 114 x 146 cm
Collection M. et Mme W. Ganz, New York

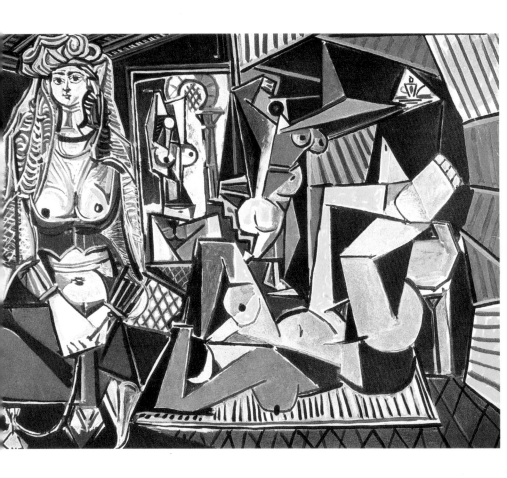

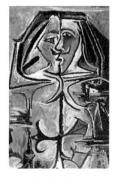

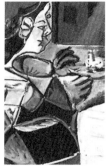

According to Pierre Daix, "Picasso always considered himself a poet who was more prone to express himself through drawings, paintings and sculptures." There is, however, no doubt that from the outset Picasso was always "a painter among poets, a poet among painters".

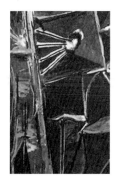

Les Ménines (after Velázquez)

1957
oil on canvas, 194 x 260
Museo Picasso, Barcelona

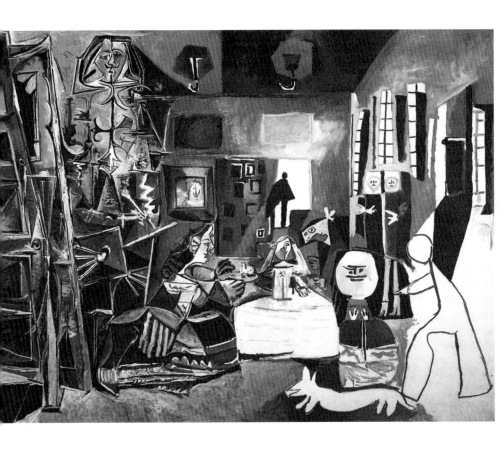

235

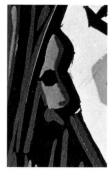

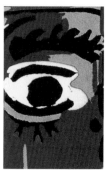

Picasso had a craving for poetry and attracted poets like a magnet.

When they first met, Apollinaire was struck by the young Spaniard's unerring ability "to straddle the lexical barrier" and grasp the fine points of recited poetry.

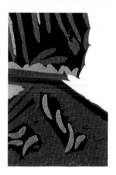

Woman with a Hat (Half-Length)

1962
engraving on linoleum, 63.5 x 52.5 cm

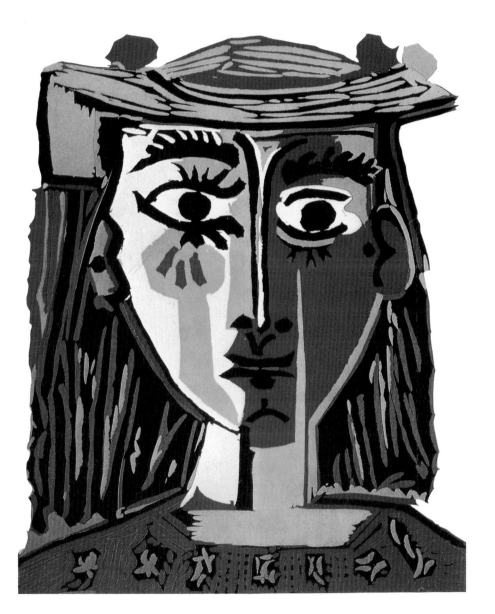

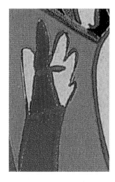

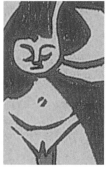

One may say without fear of exaggeration that while Picasso's close friendship with the poets Jacob, Apollinaire, Salmon, Cocteau, Reverdy and Eluard left an imprint on each of the major periods of his work, it is no less true that his own innovative work had a strong influence on French twentieth-century poetry. And this assessment of Picasso's art – so visual and obvious, yet at times so blinding, opaque and mysterious – as that of a poet, is dictated by the artist's own view of his work.

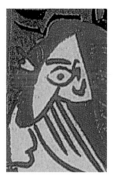

Déjeuner sur l'herbe (after Manet)

1962
engraving on linoleum, 53.3 x 64.5 cm

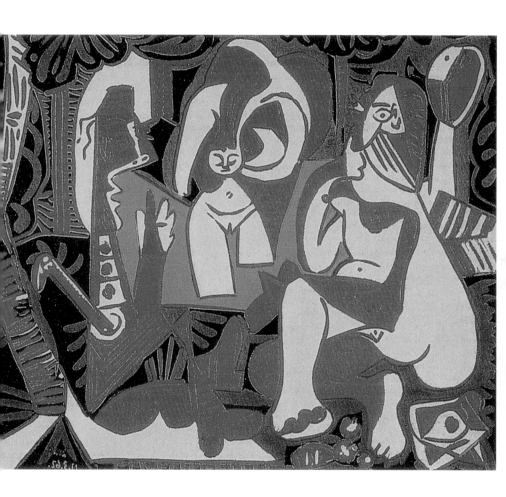

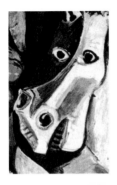

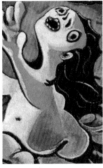

He even expressed the following thought: "If I had been born Chinese, I would not be a painter but a writer. I'd write my pictures."

In the summer and autumn of 1912, while living with Eva in the town of Sorgues-sur-l'Ouvèze, Picasso was literally possessed by one subject: some fifteen paintings of that season depict violins and guitars.

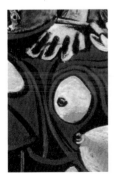

The Kidnapping of the Sabines

1963
oil on canvas, 195.5 x 130 cm
Museum of Fine Arts, Boston

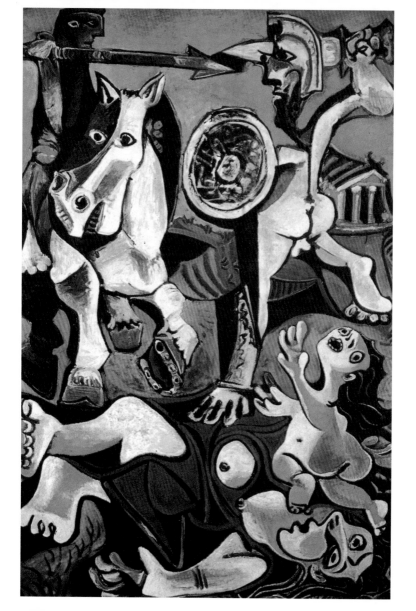

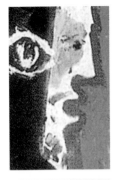

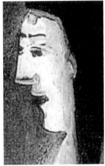

This was lyrical painting, steeped in emotions relating the shapes of these instruments to the female form and aspiring to create a harmonic and tangible image out of different elements of form, rhythm, texture, both of material and painted surface, and colour. *Still-Life with Violin* is one of Picasso's first and most harmonious works of that period.

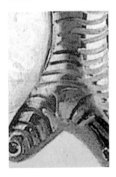

The Painter and His Model

1963
oil on canvas, 130 x 162 cm
Museo español de Arte Contemporaneo

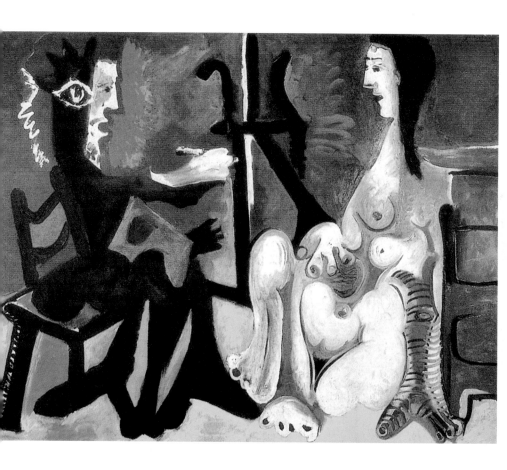

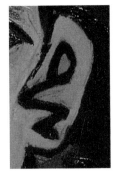

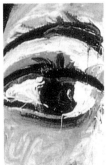

The painting can hardly be classed as a still life: its formative idea is better expressed by the words *tableau-objet*, which Picasso himself used. Musical instruments, considered a lyrical subject by Picasso, continued to occupy his imagination for many months. In the autumn of 1912, in Paris, attempting to realize his new vision, he again turned to three-dimensional sculptural forms to create a family of spatial constructions in the shape of guitars.

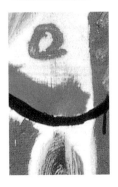

Portrait of Jacqueline

1963
oil on canvas, 92 x 60 cm
Rosengart Gallery

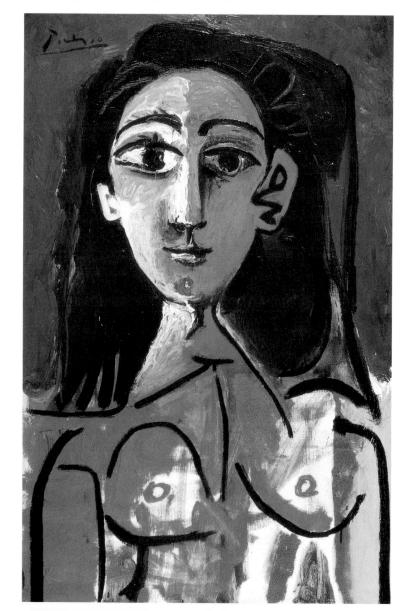

245

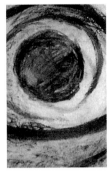

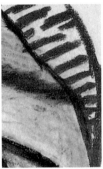

At the end of 1912, these new lyrical objects as well as the oval *tableau-objets*, destined only to hang on walls, furnished the impulse for endless new interpretations and experimentations.

Through these formal inventions, Picasso had put into practice the plastic metaphor within the frame of the painting, broadening the potentialities of art.

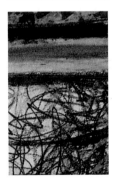

Self-Portrait (Head)

1972
pencil and crayon on paper, 65.7 x 50.5 cm
Fuji Television Gallery, Tokyo

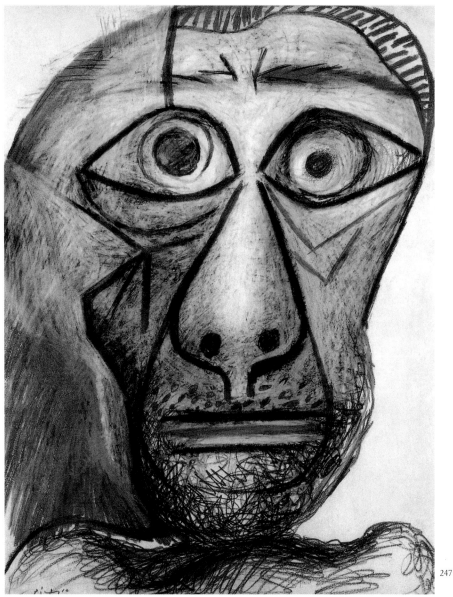

Index

A

Academic Study   11

B

Bathers   141

Bottle of Pernod and Wineglass (Table in a Café)   181

Bowl of Fruit with Bunch of Grapes and Sliced Pear   195

Bowl with Fruit and Wineglass (Still-Life with Bowl and Fruit)   155

Boy Leading a Horse   113

Boy with a Dog   79

Boy with a Pipe   95

Bunch of Flowers in a Grey Jug   153

C

Celestina   75

Chest of a Woman, Study for Les Demoiselles d'Avignon   117

Chest of a Woman, Study for Les Demoiselles d'Avignon   119

Child with a Pigeon   39

Clarinet and Violin   187

Clown with a Young Acrobat   83

Composition Bowl of Fruit and Sliced Pear   193

Composition with a Skull   127

D

Déjeuner sur l'herbe (after Manet)   239

F

Factory in Horta de Ebro   167

Family of Acrobats with a Monkey   89

Family of Saltimbanques (Comedians)   87

Figures on the Beach   211

First Communion   15

Frenzy   27

Friendship   131

Friendship   133

G

Glassware, Still-Life with a Porro   105

Green Bowl and Black Bottle   151

Guernica   223

H

Harlequin and His Companion	37
Head of a Woman with a Scarf	71
Head of an Old Man with a Crown	97
Head, Study for "Les Demoiselles d'Avignon"	121
House and Trees (House in a Garden)	149
House in a Garden (House and Trees)	161

I

Interior Scene: Nude Woman beside a Cat and a Nude Man	99

L

La Fermière (Half-Length)	135
La Toilette	101
Lady with a Fan	163
Le Gourmet	35
Le Moulin de la Galette	25
Les Demoiselles d'Avignon	123
Les Ménines	235
Life	73

M

Man with Crossed Arms   165

Mother and Child   59

Musical Instruments   189

N

Naked Boy   91

Nude (Half-Length)   115

Nude in a Landscape (The Dryad)   139

Nude Woman Sitting in an Armchair (Young Woman)   169

Nude Woman with Crossed Legs   61

O

Old Jew and a Boy   67

P

Paul as Harlequin   203

Peasant Woman (Full-Length)   145

Pierrot and a Dancer   29

Pitcher and Bowls   147

Poor People on the Seashore (The Tragedy)   69

Portrait of a Young Girl (Woman Seated Before a Fireplace)   197

Portrait of Ambroise Vollard   173

Portrait of Dora Maar   225

Portrait of Henri Kahnweiler   175

Portrait of Jacqueline   245

Portrait of Jacqueline with Flowers   231

Portrait of Marie-Thérèse Walter   219

Portrait of Soler   63

Portrait of the Artist's Father   13

Portrait of the Artist's Mother   17

Portrait of the Poet Sabartes (The Glass of Beer)   49

Poverty-Stricken Woman   57

Prostitutes at the Bar   55

Q

Queen Isabeau   157

S

Self-Portrait   19

Self-Portrait   31

Self-Portrait   51

Self-Portrait   109

Self-Portrait (Head)   247

Self-Portrait with a Palette   103

Spanish Woman from Majorca   93

Still-Life with Chair Caning   179

Study of a Nude, Seen from the Back   9

T

Tavern (The Ham),   191

The Absinthe Drinker   41

The Absinthe Drinker   43

The Bathers   199

The Bullfight   215

The Burial of Casagémas   45

The Burial of Casagémas (Evocation)   47

The Crucifixion   207

The Dance of the Veils (Nude with Draper)   125

The Embrace   21

The Kidnapping of the Sabines   241

The Kiss   205

The Lecture   213

The Painter and His Model   243

The Peace   229

The Sculptor   209

The Soler Family   65

The Supplicant   221

The Two Brothers   111

The Visit (Two Sisters)   53

The War   227

Three Women   143

Tumblers (Mother and Son)   81

Two Figures in Profile, and the Head of a Man, Studies   33

Two Naked Women   107

V

Violin   183

Violin and Guitar   185

Violin, Wineglass, Pipe and Inkpot   177

W, Y

Weeping Woman   217

Woman Reading   23

Woman Seated (Nude Woman Seated)   129

Woman seated in an Armchair   171

Woman with a Hat (Half-Length)   237

Woman with a Helmet of Hair (An Acrobat's Wife)   77

Woman with a Mandolin   159

Woman with Fan (After the Ball)   137

Women of Algiers (After Delacroix)   233

Women Running on the Beach   201

Young Acrobat on a Ball   85